SOMEBODY SAID THAT
IT COULDN'T BE DONE...

Somebody said that it couldn't be done

An entrepreneur's tale

To Tom —
Best wishes
Charles Lawrence

Charles Lawrence

Matador
9 Priory Business Park,
Wistow Road, Kibworth Beauchamp,
Leicestershire. LE8 0RX
Tel: 0116 279 2299
Email: books@troubador.co.uk
Web: www.troubador.co.uk/matador
Twitter: @matadorbooks

ISBN 978 1 8004 6512 1

British Library Cataloguing in Publication Data.
A catalogue record for this book is available from the British Library.

Printed and bound by CPI Group (UK) Ltd, Croydon, CR0 4YY
Typeset in 10pt Adobe Garamond Pro by Troubador Publishing Ltd, Leicester, UK

Matador is an imprint of Troubador Publishing Ltd

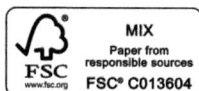

MIX
Paper from
responsible sources
FSC
www.fsc.org
FSC® C013604

This book is dedicated to my wife Vanessa, who has been by my side and supported me, both in the UK and in many countries around the world, while I was building up my business. Without her love and advice I am sure we could not have succeeded in the way we did. Always remember behind every successful man there is a good woman.

.

Contents

*

.

Foreword

Sir John Peace

I am delighted to be asked to write a foreword to a very dear friend's book.

'Someone Said It Couldn't Be Done' is the perfect title for Charles Lawrence's book. Anyone who is acquainted with Charles will agree that he is not a person who gives up easily and he certainly thrives on a challenge. I found the book an interesting and amusing read as I imagined Charles sat with a Seager's gin talking way into the night, reflecting on early recollections of his family life, research into ancestral history and about his own successful entrepreneurial career.

This book is the ideal read for any person with the work ethic to succeed and who'd like to know how to enjoy the rewards. It also gives a realistic look into the family sacrifices which occur with success; an honest account of one man's trials and sacrifices along the way but finding the perfect life balance in the end.

A very entertaining read for the budding entrepreneur.

Preface

*

O n reflection, 2013 should have been one of the happiest years of my life. Yet there I was, sitting alone in my study, listening to the clock tolling the hours and crying my heart out. That might seem strange to you when I say that I had just sold the lion's share of my business for a considerable amount of money so that my wife Vanessa and I could afford to do practically anything we fancied.

Yet it's a measure of how I felt about the business I had built up over nearly half a century of hard graft that instead of feeling elation, I felt bereft. It really was like a piece of me had been torn out and everything seemed bleak. It's never comfortable to admit weakness and there are probably those who know me a little who couldn't imagine me suffering depression for thirty minutes, let alone the best part of a year. So perhaps it's worth saying from the very start that anyone who knows me well, understands that money was never the main motivation for creating what I did.

That's not to say that I didn't enjoy having a few bob to spend, but that making money was an effect not the cause of my desire to build something. And that is also the main reason

I am writing this book. Now that I am in my eighties and with a lot of time on my hands thanks to Covid-19, I realised I wanted more than ever to try to inspire and encourage a new generation of would-be entrepreneurs. To do that I am outlining my business philosophy and recounting some of the good as well as the bad decisions I have made over the years.

Again, anyone who knows me well, will understand that I'm not doing this out of conceit or egotism but out of a genuine desire to help. It's part of my legacy, if you will. Because now that I have time to reflect on what motivated me, from my early teenage years hauling a rotavator behind me on my pedal bike, to adulthood running a large international group of companies, at the heart of everything was a desire to create something tangible – never merely to make money.

So I offer you my own story in all humility, not to say, "Look at me, aren't I clever!" but in the hope that it will provide some insights into how you, too, can build something through hard work, innovation and a stubborn desire not to be defeated. Throughout my working life, nothing has motivated me more effectively than a critic saying, "but you can't do that" as the title of the book makes clear.

It's been quite a journey, revisiting my past, looking at old black and white images and sometimes struggling to recognise faces from so many years ago. However, it has also been highly enjoyable recalling decades of experiences and clawing to retrieve some memories where a drink or two may have clouded my recollection.

But I hope you will agree with me that it has been a life well lived, peopled with good friends and plenty of love and laughs. I have had the privilege of working with some excellent individuals who should also take pride in what we achieved together. I certainly could not have done so much without you and I plan to repay it many times by helping the community in my beloved Newark.

Charles Lawrence
Newark-on-Trent 2021

Chapter One

*

Don't be afraid to take risks

If there is one lesson that my father Clifford Alfred Thomas Lawrence taught me about business, it is how important it is not to be afraid to take a risk. A flamboyant, larger than life character, he certainly lived up to that himself as a business philosophy. As I write this, he is looking down on me from his photograph on the wall and I feel reasonably confident he would give his blessing to what I've achieved. I just wish he had been around to see it.

Sadly, he died when I was only 19, so there are many gaps in my knowledge of the family on my father's side though I have been able to piece together some of the details from public records. My grandparents on my father's side were David Herbert Lawrence and Ada Maria, nee Blanchett, who married in Kensington in 1882 when he was only 21 and my grandmother was a year older, though not quite on the shelf, at 22.

Curiously, the first records I can find of my grandfather are from 1881, by which time he had left his parents' home because he is listed as living with his uncle and aunt at Woodborough Villa in Wimbledon. At that time, he gave his occupation as commercial clerk and his uncle – who was another Charles Lawrence – is listed as an army agent. Charles and his wife Felicia list their own three children on the census plus my grandfather who was born in 1861, somewhere in Middlesex, and another niece who gives her name as Jane Jeans and was then only 13 years old.

Now it's hard to know why my grandfather and Jane were being looked after by their aunt and uncle and I know speculation is idle. Nonetheless, I can't help but think that I could well be named after my great uncle Charles who clearly took my grandfather into his home when he was just starting out on his career. Maybe it was my father's way of saying thank you to his kindly great uncle for providing his father with board and lodging as part of their family.

Anyroad, my grandfather clearly had a lot of drive and by 1891 he has a family of his own and is living in Marbury Villa, Park Road, Kingston. There he is by the age of 30, with four children of his own and a new occupation – as an advertising agent. There is no record of the house today but if you're interested, you could recently have picked up a four-bedroom Georgian semi which was once called Oak Villa for fifty quid under a million pounds. Though in that era, it was far more likely my grandparents were renting.

And they certainly weren't wasting any time because the year after they were married, my grandmother gave birth to Evelyn (1883) then Sydney (1884), Stanley (1888) and Leonard (1891). For good measure they had also taken in a

German lodger by the name of Gustave Kram. What's more, my grandfather must have come on in the world because they also had two servants – 20-year-old Ada and 14-year-old Elizabeth, who is listed as a general servant domestic.

Perhaps those not familiar with Victorian norms, may be shocked to see a child labourer in my grandparents' employment. Well, I've done my homework and it was very common for youngsters to go into domestic service – particularly young girls – while they were still in their childhood. According to the 1891 census which I've just been quoting, there were 1.3 million girls and young women in domestic service around England in that year. Most were recruited between the ages of 10 and 14 after a rudimentary education in literacy and numeracy. A great many of them worked in London.

The life of any domestic servant in that era was extremely hard, working long hours to carry out some of the dirtiest and hardest tasks in the house from setting fires before the family got up, to emptying chamber pots from the previous night. Domestic servants were under constant surveillance and had very little time off, living in an apartheid system where they were *with* the family but always reminded they were not *part* of the family. My grandmother would almost certainly have had one of the many handbooks instructing her on how to treat their servants.

On the plus side, though obviously I have no idea if my grandparents were kind employers, domestic servants had somewhere to live and a meagre but regular food supply. In 1860 the law changed so employers no longer had the right to beat their domestics and though they were not allowed "callers" at the house, many left once they became engaged and started a different life of drudgery. Bear in mind too, that life was far worse for many others in the London of 1891 with some 50,000 families living in a single room and below that was the dreaded Workhouse with its barbaric atmosphere.

However, I assume my grandparents must have lived quite comfortably and by 1901 they had moved to the rather grandly named Fieldview, in Gloucester Road, Kingston-upon-Thames. By then, my grandfather was 40 and listing himself in the census of that year as an advertising agent and publisher. By that time too, Sydney, Stanley and Leonard had all been packed off to Cranleigh boarding school – where I would later suffer – and two more children had been added to the family. My father Clifford was born in 1893 and he was followed by his sister Vera, born three years later.

They had also gone up a bit in the world. My father, who was eight at the time of the 1901 census, and Vera, who was six, were being looked after by Maud Marshall, a 21-year-old described as a Nurse Housemaid. My grandmother Ada would have been far too grand to do much nappy changing or reading bedside stories and clearly didn't do any cooking. Also on the census is 25-year-old Beatrice Newton, who is down as the Cook General. Things must have been looking pretty good from the front windows of Fieldview, but then they had no idea of the family tragedy that was soon to engulf them all.

Today, even during the lockdown which followed the COVID-19 pandemic, you can still take a trip along Gloucester Road thanks to Google Maps and you can see that there are still plenty of solid brick-built detached and semi-detached houses from the era when my father would have been growing up there. Much of it has been redeveloped and it seems "Fieldview" will have had to change its name to "Urbanview", because there is precious little open land anywhere in the area.

The biggest event for my eight-year-old father would have been the death of the 81-year-old Queen Victoria after 64 years on the throne, during a period when Britain had dominated the world in manufactures and territory. She was succeeded in 1901 by her 59-year-old playboy son who became King Edward VII and ushered in the Edwardian era. While the economy was still booming, it was a time of change and progress particularly in science.

Marconi broadcast the first trans-Atlantic wireless signal and the first vacuum cleaner was patented. Thanks to the Factory and Workshop Act the minimum working age was raised to 12 – just four years older than my father was at the time. And the country had been through a century of unparalleled transition with 85 per cent of the British people now living in urban areas as opposed to 15 per cent just over a century before.

Then just when everything must have been looking bright, the family was hit by disaster. It's clear from the records that in 1906, when he was only 45 years old, my grandfather died. It says nothing on the certificate about cause of death, but it must have been a massive shock for his widow and all the children. Losing my own father when I was 19 was a terrible blow. My father lost his when he was only 13. He will probably have received the news when he was away at school in Cranleigh with his brothers. It certainly helps to understand why he was so determined to live his life to the full.

By the time of the next census, my grandmother is listed as the head of the house and a widow living off private means. Her eldest daughter, Evelyn, has been married off so sharing the new house at 17 Gloucester Road are my uncles Stanley (23), Leonard (20), my father Clifford (18) and the youngest daughter Vera (16). My grandmother who had been widowed for five years was only 51. There are times when you look at old records, stained and discoloured with age and they can cause the same pain and awful sense of sadness and loss as at the time of the event.

The honest truth is that until I began this project, I had very little knowledge of my father's family other than a jolly old Uncle Stanley who filled the part of being a director of Watney's Brewery, with his big white moustache and his lah-di-dah posh accent. But it seems fair to assume that the terrible early death of my grandfather must have been a huge spur to my father, who went on to have a very successful business career. But I get ahead of myself; let me fill you in with some of the background of my father's life before and after my grandfather died.

What I do know is, that along with his brothers, he was sent to Cranleigh – a private school in Surrey. There he would certainly have distinguished himself at cricket – a lifelong passion. Like all the boys, he would also have done his time in the Officers Training Corps which was founded in 1900 when the Boer War was at its height. Please note that Cranleigh only prepared its alumni to become officers, so the group was called the Swagger Stick, after the baton that officers carried. Later renamed the Combined Cadet Force, it was in essence where young men dressed as soldiers and played at war. They can have had little intimation of the impending catastrophe of the First World War which was about to engulf them and steal a large proportion of the young men of my father's generation.

The records show that he duly enlisted in 1915 at the age of 22 as Second Lieutenant Lawrence of the East Surrey Regiment and clearly distinguished himself enough to end the conflict as Captain Lawrence. Like so many men of that era, it was not something he talked much about. But I can't help feeling that the experiences he went through and the fact that he survived the conflict when so many of his contemporaries never came home would have dramatically coloured his outlook on life. Now let me tell you how he came to survive.

This is where I take my metaphorical hat off to all those who have done fantastic work digitising millions of written records – in this case from the First World War. Thanks to the Surrey History Centre, I discovered that my father was with the 8th Battalion of the East Surrey Regiment and after officer training, was despatched to France on May 24th, 1916. But here is where the records leave you wanting more: let me just say that he duly arrived in France but was not destined to stay for long and within two weeks was on his way home. To put it mildly that was highly unusual so let me share with you what the records say.

The meticulously typed daily log prepared by Captain Cecil Clare of the 8th Battalion details exactly what was happening during the time my father was actually in France. He was extremely fortunate in that the men he was joining had just survived a gruelling six-week stint in the trenches on the Front Line. The battalion – which at full strength would have been just over 1000 men – had made the march back without loss and had arrived in the Picquigny billeting area for rest and training on May 4th. Luckily for my father, they spent the following day bathing and cleaning their equipment, because after a stint in the trenches, they would all have stunk to high heaven and been covered in lice.

In the fortnight before Second Lieutenant Clifford Lawrence reported for duty, his battalion was getting ready for a period of intense training near the Bois du Gard some miles behind the front line. Just before he got there, he had missed a full day of bayonet exercises, rapid loading and the exercise beloved by every soldier – a route march. Just for good measure, they were accompanied on the march by transport, pack ponies, carts and spare transport. No escape for anyone.

On the day he joined his battalion, it was still pretty quiet with a detachment of 80 men sent off on barge fatigue which meant either unloading supplies from canal barges or loading the wounded for their journey home. The day after his arrival on May 25th he may have had a taste of trench warfare, though only on the training ground where they will have practised the drill for going "over the top" for an attack. After a day practising the attack, they were given a new billet at Fourdinoy where my father will have spent his second night in France. It's so odd to think of my 23-year-old father trying to find his place in this chaotic and confusing new reality.

At least officers will have been spared the work of digging latrines and making incinerators for their rubbish, but once that was out of the way, it was time for a bit of fun. On May 26th there was a sports day with a tug of war at which the 8th Battalion excelled, under the watchful gaze of a swagger of generals, both British and French. (I know that's not the official term for a group of top brass, but it seemed appropriate!) Then it was straight back into three days of gruelling training for trench warfare, including the frightening prospect of drills for poison gas which had already claimed many casualties.

Forgive me quoting this in some detail, but when you read these calmly written reports it's impossible for us, in a time of peace, to picture what it was like for men like my father, who up until then, had barely left the comforts of the family home. Early June began with the same relentless training regime and then his battalion had the honour of being inspected on the 3rd by the head of British forces in France, General Sir Douglas Haig. If only I'd had a chance to talk to my father about it.

Depending on how ill he was by now, his last day with the battalion was practising what was described as an "abnormal attack" in trenches laid out to resemble the German front line. It was hampered by heavy rain, but the report says the men did better once they had had their food and tried again in the afternoon. I can only assume that many of them secretly envied my father because the records clearly say he was too sick to stay in France. What they don't say is what he was suffering from. The only observation I would make is it must have been pretty serious – the British Army was not known for being soft hearted in the First World War.

However, as he was being transported back to England, the unit with which he had just become acquainted were already back in the trenches. By June 11th, when he was crossing the Channel, they were under heavy enemy bombardment. Unless he was delirious, what on earth was he thinking about? Did he know how fortunate he was to escape the slaughter or was he bitter that he had missed his first chance of glory?

I ask the question because three days later, by which time he would have been safely housed back in a British hospital, two second lieutenants from his battalion were among the dead in a huge German bombardment. One died immediately, the other from his injuries. Nine NCOs and privates were also killed, and many others wounded. The shelling and the casualties continued until they were finally relieved and could go back down the line on June 20th for a bath and some hot food. Maybe once my father had fully recovered, he went back to his old school to give them a taste of what they could expect if they joined up.

Even though Cranleigh was not a particularly big establishment, it did suffer a disproportionately heavy casualty rate, like so many of the British public schools. The death toll among young officers was particularly high as they were expected to lead their men over the top, in often suicidal attacks. In all, my father was one of 1,300 Cranleigh old boys and masters who fought in World War One and 201 of them died, including ten who had gone straight from school. Fortunately, my father was one of those who made it through and, given the shortage of adult males, he could take his pick of careers once he had been demobbed.

Though he started life as a banker with the now defunct Baring Brothers bank, he soon established his own business trading in foreign currency. Lawrence Brothers, which he ran with the assistance of his brother Leonard, was a success and my father became a well-known figure in the City of London. Information is scarce but I can safely assume that at the same time, he was taking full advantage of all the pleasures London had to offer in those hedonistic inter-war years.

So, it must have come as a nasty shock when, with the threat of the Second World War, all foreign exchange dealings were suspended in 1938. However, it's also the measure of the man and the reason I say he was never afraid to take risks in business that he immediately reinvented himself as a hotelier. Unless you count his days as a paying guest at the Dorchester Hotel in London, he had absolutely no practical experience of the hospitality industry.

What's more, despite the fact that his life was very much focused on London for both business and pleasure, he had married Peggy Eileen Taylor in 1931. Before the marriage, my mother had been working on the Elizabeth Arden counter at the main Boots branch in Nottingham though it's more likely they met at the Clinton Arms where my maternal grandfather worked. The wedding took place in Newark and, knowing my father's penchant for the good life, would probably have been rather a grand affair. Equally, he spent enough time with her to father his first child – my sister was born on August 7th the following year in Newark and christened Valerie Anne.

Being an impetuous kind of guy, my father had already bought the best hotel in Newark and now with his foreign exchange business closed, he embarked on his new career as a full-time hotelier. It's funny as I look at him in his photograph to think what Newark would have made of him when he roared up the A1 in his open top sportscar and came to a halt in the lovely town square where the building of the Clinton Arms Hotel still sits proudly.

In his photo he comes across as someone who enjoyed a gamble – maybe, again, to do with losing his father so young and his experience in the war – and a man very fond of the good things in life. Whatever the Prince of Wales had, he had to have too, whether that was gold cufflinks, a gold lighter or the best Savile Row suits. Everywhere he went, he cut quite a dash and he was determined to bring all the pleasures of London life to Newark. There's a cartoon of him in the Daily Sketch – a newspaper which was closed in 1971 and merged with the more successful Daily Mail – which illustrates the "characters of Newark" in 1936 and my father was certainly one of them.

My oldest friend, Geoffrey Bond, has some very strong memories of my father, even when he was a youngster. He describes him as an extraordinary man with big beetling eyebrows who was always beautifully dressed – very much as I have already said. He also says he was a bit of a disciplinarian, by which I assume he meant he ran a pretty tight ship at the Clinton Arms. But he also has strong recollections of my mother who he also remembers as a commanding presence and an impressive character. Well, they did preside over the swankiest hotel in town!

It's a bit sad, but I would love to suggest you take a tour round the place today; you will find a very different and less glamorous site. Gone is the great glassed-over lounge with its palm trees and cane chairs. Although some of the original flooring is still there, it's now all boutiques and banks. Where the public bar used to welcome customers, you will find a branch of the Spanish owned bank Santander. The town square is as handsome as ever, but it's all gone a bit Starbucks and BetFred. I know nothing stays the same, but I don't think my father would have approved.

Nor would my mother – always known to the family as Tootie – who certainly did know how to make an entrance and loved her big hats and loud, brightly-coloured clothes.

For those of you familiar with the history of the 1950's, she always reminded me a bit of the extraordinary socialite and controversial figure Lady Docker, who was married at the time to the extremely wealthy Sir Bernard. Now I don't think my mother loved the limelight as much as Lady Docker did, and I am certain my mother had far fewer enemies!

Above all, my mother loved flower arranging and would put on training courses, no doubt for the local Women's Institute meetings. As a result of that, and her position at the Clinton Arms, everybody knew Peggy. Her love of flowers also meant that the hotel was always lavishly bedecked with elaborate floral decorations which contributed a lot to the grandeur of the place and must have made it smell nice too.

The Clinton Arms came with a fair bit of history as there had been a hotel on that site since at least the 15th century, although the elegant façade visible in 1938 was largely that of the coaching inn built in the 18th century for passengers of the stagecoach.

According to the records, the notorious poet Lord Byron – he of mad, bad and dangerous to know fame – stayed in the hotel in 1806 to oversee the publication of his very first collection of poems which were being printed just across the market square at the shop of one Mr Ridge.

The Clinton Arms also found fame as the political headquarters of one of Britain's most famous prime ministers – the Liberal party leader William Ewart Gladstone when seeking his first parliamentary seat in 1832. He was duly elected in December of that year and remained MP for Newark for the next fourteen years, as well as going on to serve as Prime Minister of Britain and Ireland four times between 1868 and 1894.

Mr Gladstone had a reputation for being a bit dour – Queen Victoria couldn't stand him – so I can't help but wonder what he would have made of my father. Especially as there is a photograph of my father in the market square, standing outside the hotel. In another we see his AC Sports car and Talbot limousine, the Daimler of its day, which his chauffeur drove up to Newark from London. Certainly, that fondness for a bit of luxury and speed must have rubbed off on me because one of my earliest ambitions was to have my own Rolls Royce by the age of 30 – you will have to read on to find out whether or not I achieved that particular aim.

There was one other guest of note at the hotel who had close links with Newark and the surrounding area – that was General Vladislav Sikorski, the wartime Polish Prime Minister in exile and head of the Polish Armed Forces. General Sikorski was a great advocate of Polish independence and large numbers of Polish fighter pilots were flying from the RAF bases during the Second World War. When Sikorski died in a mysterious plane crash returning from Gibraltar, he was initially buried in the Polish War Graves cemetery in Newark.

It was only fifty years later that his body was flown back to a free and independent Poland for a state burial, but rumours continued to circulate that Stalin's people had been behind the plane crash. That was why the Poles carried out a full forensic examination. The bodies of three other Polish officers, who had been killed in the crash and were buried in Newark, were also taken back to Poland for a post-mortem but there was no evidence of poison or suspicious death.

Anyway, Sikorski was certainly a guest at the hotel and it's fair to say the war years were the heyday of the Clinton Arms hotel with its 39 bedrooms and men only private bar. And there was never any doubt who ruled the roost there whether he was entertaining Polish prime ministers, American and British officers or just his chums in the bar and the lounge or eating the gourmet offerings in the dining room. My father was like the captain of his own ship, resplendent in his suits and respected – maybe even feared – by his crew.

The next bit all happened in a bit of a blur but let me give you the fuzzy outlines, for it is time for me to enter my own narrative. When my sister was six years old, Charles Clifford Seager Lawrence emerged with a lusty cry at Newark Hospital on February 1st, 1939. Now I really can't claim much of the credit for any of this, but it was an age when to have a male heir was even more important than keeping the front parlour spotless. So, I can only assume that my parents were both relieved and proud – something they would continue to show for as long as they lived and, for which, I am eternally grateful.

Coincidentally, it was about this time that the Great Depression officially ended after it had run its course over the previous decade bringing more misery than any other downturn until the present day. My birth was also shortly before the end of the Spanish civil war and weeks away from Germany's invasion of Czechoslovakia on March 15th. Radio was the dominant medium and modern music flourished, particularly jazz and the big band sound.

A detached house in a good area would set you back £1,000, Ford had introduced a small saloon car for £500 for which a gallon of petrol would cost you two shillings, a bottle of milk was 1.5 old pennies and if you were a clerical worker you would pay for it all from your princely weekly wages of around £5 – less for a manual worker. Oh and for the record, in that pre-decimal era, there were 12 old pence to the shilling and twenty shillings to the pound.

It was the year which saw the first appearance of the Batman character in comics and August welcomed the arrival of the film The Wizard of Oz. Meanwhile, young Charles slept through it all, unaware that his star sign was Aquarius which was supposed to mean he would turn out gregarious and humanitarian as well as stubborn and uncompromising. Not a bad prediction, given that I don't have much time for astrology.

Although we had a large flat with an enormous Buckingham Palace-sized drawing room in the hotel, my father had rented a lovely house called Manor Cottage in Hawton, a few miles south of Newark. A few hundred yards from the village church and near the riverside, it would be my father's house until he died and remained my mother's home for another sixty years. Today, it has doubled in size and though the extension is very much in keeping with the original design, it just doesn't have the same sympathetic resonance as in my memories. It's not worse, it's just different.

What's more, though I don't have any real recollection of those war years, it was clear that my mother took well to her new role as wife, mother and chatelaine of the hotel and the house. It must have meant a huge change from everything she had previously known, but her nature was a happy mix of determination and sweetness which certainly had a profound effect on how I turned out. Well, I certainly got the determination and I'll let you judge about the sweetness.

Now this may seem odd to those who've only viewed World War Two from books and black and white films, but when I reflect on the period from 1939 to 1945, I have only a jumbled and somewhat fuzzy rag bag of memories. Being in Newark, we were right in the middle of the war effort with RAF landing fields and army bases all around. Some of my earliest memories are of a Lancaster bomber crash landing in a nearby field and Spitfires and Hurricanes making fast and sometimes desperate efforts to make it down safely.

Yet I have no recollection of being afraid. The adults would never have voiced their own misgivings in front of the children when things were going badly. And thanks to the hotel, I have no memory of any shortages or difficulties getting supplies. There were bombing raids and a large ball

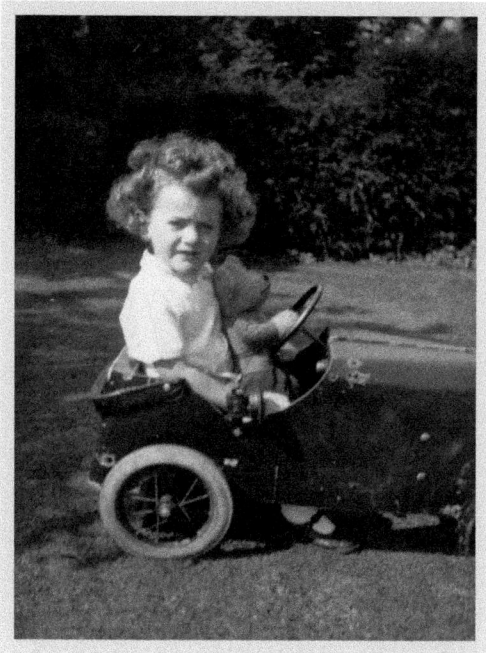

In my pedal car aged two when I was known as Bubbles

Aged two with my sister Valerie and mother Peggy

bearing factory in the centre of Newark received a direct hit with all the ensuing casualties just half a mile from the hotel. But we remained safe.

In fact, in some regards we were unusually well off. A close friend of the family who was my godfather was also the proprietor of the Seager's gin company. In return for christening me Seager as one of my middle names, my father was guaranteed an unlimited supply of this fine beverage and, as a result, was able to supply all the local officers' messes as well as keeping a steady flow going at the Clinton Arms.

Not surprisingly, the hotel bar was the 'go to' place for all the local officers and my father was a very popular and well recognised figure – not just for his access to the gin, but because he was indeed a hugely entertaining individual. He was just what his clientele needed as a distraction from what was going on every day when they would all have realised they might not be coming back.

It was very much run as a family hotel. My father was called Mr Clifford by all the staff and I was universally known as Master Charles. Part of the ceremony and charm of the place was that every day at noon my father would walk into the Gentlemen's bar in a double-breasted suit wearing his MCC tie. He would bow to the assembled company and say, "Good morning gentlemen." Everyone in the room would chorus back "Good morning Mr Clifford." Quite the showman.

The bar also played host to a motley crew of local characters such as Robert Kiddey, the noted painter and sculptor who always wore a green pork pie hat. Another was George Kimber, famed as the finest auctioneer of sheep in Nottinghamshire, who took his daily breakfast in the bar consisting of two large gins and a bunch of grapes. Cyril Parlby, then the editor of the Newark Advertiser, said the best stories in his paper tended to originate in this most exclusive of watering holes.

As for the staff, for a long time I could clearly picture their faces and mannerisms. In the kitchen there were Mr Ball and – appropriately enough – Mrs Cook. Bissie was the waitress and Tom Freeman was the footman. Robert Taylor managed the garage and I recall that he always wore a grey trilby hat and had a distinctive white moustache. One of the young mechanics, John Heron, began his career as a Rolls Royce apprentice and went on to establish the Heron dealership.

Now, along with running the hotel, my father was also divisional controller for the local Home Guard during the Second World War. Given his years of experience in the First

World War, he took it very seriously. Though to be honest, the real appeal for him and his fellow Home Guard officers was to have lengthy strategy meetings on how best to defend Newark from the Nazis in the bar of the hotel. In fairness, whatever the strategy was, it appears to have worked and although some of you may have had your opinions of the Home Guard entirely formed by the television programme Dad's Army, as far as my dad and his mates were concerned, I think they would have been more than a match for any invader. Though it's just as well we never had to find out.

Once the Americans entered the war in November 1942, the hotel – particularly the bar – was even busier. Though my father was always most particular about who he allowed in, and although most of them would end up rather tight, there was never any trouble. Despite the war, my upbringing was a largely untroubled idyll of calm. What a pity it had to change – but more of that later.

The Americans set up a huge anti-aircraft battery in the woods near the town and I can remember going past the guns. Then the local army units started practising building Bailey bridges across the local river in preparation for what became the D-Day landings in France. Though curiously, the hard work always seemed to end up with a hearty session involving a lot of Seager's gin.

I'm indebted to Geoffrey Bond again for his recollection of one of our earliest meetings when we were only four or five and the end of the war was in sight. He claims a vivid memory of me as an extremely pretty, very curly haired boy who was, like him, extremely mischievous. It seems we were dragged by our respective mothers to a dance school and apparently we were both kicked out after pulling the girls' pigtails. Maybe it was a portent of our future relationships with womankind. It certainly explains my lifelong aversion to dancing and dance floors.

You would also think that something as momentous as the end of World War Two would have left a lasting impression on a young mind. However, when the war ended I was six years old. I do remember being at a victory celebration in London and I can also recall being dressed up in a kilt to lead a military parade in the market square of Newark. However, as the war came to an end my life was about to change completely and not for the better. In the rather brutal fashion of the time, I was about to be separated from my family and packed off to boarding school. Not exactly Dickens' terrifying image of Dotheboys Hall in Nicholas Nickleby, but probably the unhappiest time of my life.

Chapter Two

*

Know your strengths

My years of formal education began in a makeshift classroom above a Chemists Shop in the centre of Newark. To all intents and purposes, they might just as well have ended there. It's clear to me that my business career is proof that I'm not stupid. But the next ten years in the jungles of academe were an uphill slog in an ill-fitting pair of shoes. It finally came to an end with the equivalent of a resounding 'nul points' in the Eurovision Song Contest.

Don't get me wrong, I'm not saying that an education is not a very good – in fact essential – rite of passage. What I am saying is that if you let other people, or a system, define you then you are never going to make the most of what your real talents are. Nobody was ever going to give me a diploma in tractor maintenance or a degree in ploughing but my fascination with tractors (friends would say love affair) was part of what inspired me to do what I have subsequently achieved.

Maybe in some ways, it was easier in my day to be successful without a double first in Politics, Philosophy and Economics from Oxbridge. After all, the Beatles weren't formed in the Magdalen College common room. And looking at how things are now, it does seem to me that for this generation the bar for getting started has been raised incredibly high. For many top jobs, young people need a good degree as the minimum entrance requirement.

But being an entrepreneur is a very different thing. It can't be any coincidence that Richard Branson is a self-confessed dyslexic who never graduated. Come to that, neither did Bill Gates of Microsoft or Mark Zuckerberg of Facebook fame and it certainly didn't do either of them any harm. While I wouldn't necessarily compare myself to any of those luminaries, the basic driving force is the same and to succeed you have to know your own strengths.

However, I digress. Let me take you back to the classroom above the Chemists shop where my own academic journey began. Today Highfields School is a very successful co-educational, non-selective independent day school for children from 2 to 11 – one of the best in Newark. Back in the days after the Second World War had ended, it was a very different story. Things were so scarce we had to go to school with our own chair to sit on and our own knife and fork if we wanted to eat.

My father was one of the original investors and I remain a shareholder to this day – though sadly I can't cash the shares in. Altogether, there were about 20 children from Newark in a single room, most of whom were the sons of local shopkeepers and builders. During my two terms there and throughout the rest of my school life, I maintained a clean record and never passed a single exam. While I may not be massively proud of that, you have to salute my consistency.

All that was about to change anyway – and not for the better. First, I was taken to hospital to have my tonsils out and then I was put in the charge of a private tutor to prepare me for Cranleigh School in Surrey, the alma mater of my father and his brothers. In these more child-centric days, parents might even wonder if such an option were the right one for their offspring. For me, the sentence was already passed before the trial had even begun. Cranleigh it was. The school motto should have been enough to warn me about what was to come next – "Ex Cultu Robur" – from culture comes strength. It should have read: "from beating and bullying come strength of character".

Now I'm not looking for any sympathy, but I would ask you to reflect on this. One moment, there I was, a happy, easy going seven-year-old with a loving mother, devoted father and a caring sister just six years older than me. The next, we were boarding an LNER steam train for the journey to London, my trunk in the luggage van and my head somewhere in the clouds or in the farmland near Manor Cottage. I'm indebted to the author Louis de Bernieres who has recently talked about the miseries he suffered and has called boarding schools an orphanage for children with parents – I'm with you there Louis.

Anyway, after lunch in town, we were off to Waterloo Station where I was handed over to a school master with less ceremony than you might expect as a brown paper parcel for the journey to Cranleigh. My mother waved me off and I was not to set eyes on any of my family for the next 14 weeks. If your ideas about boarding school are exclusively based on reading J.K. Rowling and feasts at Hogwarts, then allow me to enlighten you.

Without fear of contradiction, I can say this was the start of the most miserable ten years of my life. I absolutely hated school with its culture of beatings and bullying, the lousy food and the rock-hard beds. Fortunately for me I was a survivor and that inner strength allowed me to get through the experience largely undamaged – though my backside might not agree. Like I said, I'm not looking for any sympathy, but you will understand why I shed a few tears.

Having said that, I would also have to admit that school did help to form my character. On the plus side, it made me far more self-reliant – a vital aspect of entrepreneurial business success. On the less positive side, anyone who has ever disappointed me or tried to cross me in the world of business will know that I don't suffer fools. A lot of that – the angels and demons of my personality – I can trace to those grim days at boarding school.

Now you may think I am exaggerating how awful those post war years at boarding school could be. But I am highly indebted to the excellent work of the Cranleigh historian Martin Williamson – himself a Cranleigh old boy – and his excellent book "Cranleigh, the First 150 years." If anything, when I read his chapter on the Post-war years 1945 to 1970, life at school was even grimmer than I remember. At that time, the school was headed by the impressively impassive figure of one Rev David Loveday who held the office for 23 years from 1931 to 1954. Although enrolment numbers had started to rise, the school was perennially short of cash to maintain the existing buildings, let alone create anything new.

Me, aged seven, with my father and mother, ready to go to Cranleigh School

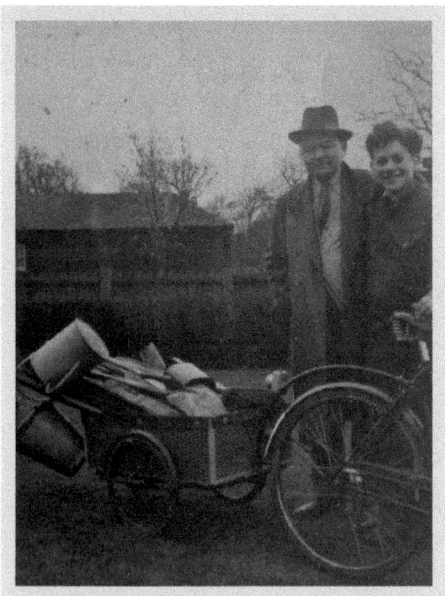

Me and my father with my bike and trailer aged 17

When I began life at Cranleigh, the war still cast a shadow over everything. Rationing didn't end until 1953 and the food we were given at school reflected that. Used to a life in the Clinton Arms Hotel where nothing was in short supply even during the war, I had to get accustomed to whatever the school kitchen could dream up by way of stews and overcooked vegetables. Friday it was fish – allegedly. Mr Williamson – who has studied the archive – says that in the summer of 1946 the housemasters collectively warned that the boys were underfed, and physical exercise would have to be reduced if the food did not improve. The idea of sport being curtailed would have been heresy at Cranleigh, so things must have been serious.

The system then was that meals were eaten in the refectory and the food was passed down the table so that the senior boys got as much as they wanted and the juniors at the end of the table had to make do with whatever was left. We were so hungry that even an endless diet of tapioca, semolina and beetroot didn't stop us eating whatever we could. Though we drew the line at tripe – which for those who are not acquainted with the delicacy is the stomach of a cow and it's very rubbery. Many were the days, we younger boys had to fill up with bread.

Back then, the annual fees were £145 for boarders though that soared 51 per cent by 1950 to £249 a year. Just to give you some modern context, today the fees are over £35,000 a year – plus extras. Also, numbers then were much lower with just 325 boys in the senior school and 74 in the prep school in 1945. By 2015 there were 626 in the senior school and 332 at the prep school. Even more significant by way of a change, 229 of them were girls. Sadly, not in my day.

In the prep school, we slept in a dormitory of around 15 boys under the baleful glare of Matron and her sister the Deputy Matron. To be fair, maybe they had not had happy lives themselves which was why they took it out on us – a motley crew of snot-nosed seven-year-olds who had never left home before and probably, like me, would regularly cry themselves to sleep. On the other hand, who wants to be fair since – not to put too fine a point on it – Matron was a miserable old cow.

You know it's funny but there is one incident from my time in the junior school which still bothers me. Utterly unfairly, I was accused of taking a bar of chocolate and I can tell you whoever did take it, that boy certainly was not me. However, I was prevailed upon to take the rap, so I did. Although the inevitable beating from the headmaster hurt, what hurt far more was the sense of injustice that I was falsely accused and punished. Some time later, the headmaster did make it known to my parents that he really didn't think I had anything to do with it which was some comfort. But it does help me understand my own sense of the importance of fairness in business and always listening to opposing arguments.

At that time, most of the punishments, including the beatings, were carried out by prefects rather than staff and we all dreaded that we would be called to a senior prefect's bathroom during prep because that almost certainly meant you were in for a beating. The usual outcome was six of the best with a bamboo cane on your bare backside, which I can quite understand now sounds terribly barbaric, but the challenge was not to return until the tears had stopped. And you wonder why I can be a tough old grizzly sometimes…

What's more, I did find some consolation in my love of gardening. Just to the side of the school, there were a dozen small patches where, if you were interested, you could cultivate your own garden. That was where I could find some escape from the rigours of the school regime. That small patch was my haven, and, with hindsight, I can see how it helped me form the idea that I would one day be a farmer – as long as the farm had tractors.

Interestingly enough, the one significant investment made by the school in 1947 was to buy William Gatley's farm at High Upfold, adjoining the school's existing grounds. The idea was two-fold: the first was to produce fresh produce for the school and the second was to encourage the boys to become interested in agriculture. You have to bear in mind that agriculture was a far bigger part of the British economy – especially for employment – than in our current, far more mechanised age. However, for the record, the farm failed in both its principal aims apart from giving me a taste for farming.

At 11 or 12 we moved to the senior school and there everything centred on your house. I was in Two North under the command of the House Master and the Head Boy. While the prep school had been a bit more relaxed, the senior school was run on military lines – these are the rules and you had better follow them or you're in serious trouble. Funnily enough, in the stern disciplinary atmosphere of Cranleigh at that time, even the farm could be used as a form of punishment for the boys – digging up the potatoes and bagging them was one of the least popular activities. Though I must have been one of the minority of boys who loved the freedom the farm could offer.

My other great escape was during the holidays. From the age of 12 or 13 I was already interested in doing agricultural work to earn some money. In my teens, I prevailed upon my father to help me set up my own first business – keeping chickens and selling the eggs. It was called Clinton Park Holdings and my father taught me all the basics about how to run a successful business including profit margins and book-keeping. It wasn't very glamorous, but it was the first real signpost for me of where I wanted to head in life, and I knew how I was going to get there – by tractor.

In the meantime, I settled for a lawnmower. My father and I would visit a horticultural machinery depot in Nottingham which was the nearest place to paradise I could imagine as a boy. Surrounded by all the wonders of British manufactured agricultural engineering, my father and I got very friendly with the owner of the store. Fortunately for me, my parents already owned an Atco 16inch DL mower. My goodness, how I cherished that machine. You're going to think I'm a total nutter, but I even installed headlights on that mower and began the – not wholly cerebral – business of mowing grass. Heaven.

What came next was an even more sublime creation from the world of British – and they were then all British-made – engineering. Always keen to encourage me and keeping any misgivings to himself, my father bought me a Howard rotavator. Made in Stamford and magnificent in its orange livery, that machine was loaded into a small trailer and pulled behind my bicycle so I could rotavate people's gardens for the sheer love of it. Well, it was for cash actually, I think I just got a bit carried away there.

It was bloody hard work, but I was utterly in my element.

It meant that when I finally left school with a huge sigh of relief and not a single piece of paper to my name, I already knew what I wanted to do with the rest of my life – become a farmer. I like to think that although my father might have been disappointed that I was not more academic, he never reproached me and indeed, seemed to take great pride in the fact that his son was proving so hard working and enterprising.

Geoffrey Bond and I became reacquainted about the time I escaped from the scholastic gulag and we adopted a lovely old pub in Newark called the Old White Hart as our meeting point. If you haven't visited the place, you really should as it's in a medieval timber-framed building considered of national architectural importance. It's thought the original structure was a merchant or wealthy craftsman's house which was converted into a pub in the 14th century – though I have to admit that we went more for the ale than the architecture.

There is one other story about the place I'd like to share with you. During the English Civil War, Newark was being besieged by parliamentary forces when a "grenado" or bomb was thrown by the besiegers and exploded in the pub. A large part of the building was blown up and some died while others were mortally wounded. I'm glad to say that the biggest danger we ever experienced there was from the amount of passive smoking we did in the cramped and crowded interior.

Now my father was certainly not one to begrudge anyone a share in the pleasures of life. But now I think about it, it's maybe surprising that he didn't even reproach me for my lack of sporting prowess at school. Frankly, I never saw the point of putting so much effort into something that didn't even pay you money. My father on the other hand was passionate about cricket and was a lifelong member of the Marylebone Cricket Club – the MCC – wearing its distinctive tie and enjoying the Long Room at Lords Cricket Ground.

Come to that, he was still enjoying all the fruits of London life, regularly travelling the 126 miles down the A1 to what was effectively his second home – the Dorchester Hotel in Park Lane, Mayfair. Nowadays, the hotel which bills itself as the 'Gold Standard of Care' will provide you with a superior room for a trifling £870 a night. For my father, who as I have already said, wanted the best of everything, the comfort and level of service would have far outweighed anything as vulgar as the cost. The other thing worth mentioning to those of you who are used to endless traffic jams and congestion is that the first motorway was only built in 1958 so his driving experience was closer to that of Mr Toad than today's prisoners of the M25 parking lot.

My father was such a fixture in the hotel that he was universally known to the staff of the Dorchester as Mr Lawrence. It always amused me when he would send the hall porter out for his Gold Flake cigarettes – classic Indian cigarettes, manufactured by W.D. and H.O. Wills and sold in their distinctive gold packet. There were certainly no health warnings on the packet in my father's day and, like many of his generation, he was rarely without one.

Anyway, he was very happy to buy me a farm by way of an investment and I was really looking forward to my future away from anything academic. So, the first thing for me to do was to get some serious farming experience and I got a job with a local landowner. I had already worked most of my holidays on a friend's family farm – needless to say, it involved driving a tractor. Now, I was going to do it full time, not realising that everything was about to change for the worse again.

My first job was for a local farmer who seemed a decent sort of chap. Around that time I bought a James Auto-cycle to get to work and back. Now here's a bit of engineering history for you. The James Motorcycle Company made motorbikes from 1897 to 1966 when, like many other British companies, they were forced out of business by Japanese competition. My auto-cycle was a 98cc wonder with a bent front fork so I had to drive it with my right hand forward a bit so it would go in a straight line.

However, what then happened was a travesty of justice and good sense which has left me even more determined to be utterly fair to my own employees if there is an issue. In essence, when the farmer was away, his son decided to sack me for not coming to work. I tried to explain to him that I was, by agreement, on holiday but he was a pig-headed individual who didn't want to listen. With hindsight, he did me a favour because it brought me closer to working for myself, though I had one other employer first.

Around that time, I started working for a farmer called Desseurn who was wasted as a farmer because he was actually a brilliant mechanic and engineer. It was a slightly eccentric set up and he had a house full of tools. What's more, I acquired a former US military left-hand drive Willys Jeep of the kind immortalised in films about the Second World War. Mr Desseurn was such a brilliant mechanic that he was able to rebuild the gearbox for me and even fixed my rotavator once.

Having access to a car stood me in excellent terms with my friends, especially for Friday evening trips to Nottingham though I may have taken the odd short cut through the shopping arcade in Newark Market Square. However, my day of judgement was about to come when it came to the highway and in the meantime, my family and I were to suffer one of the most traumatic events of my young life.

Heartbreakingly for all of us, when I was only 19, my world fell in. The loss of a parent is a trauma that almost everyone has to face eventually, but my father's death, when he was only in his early sixties, shook me to the core. Though I would remain very close to my mother until she passed away at the turn of the millennium, I now had to come to terms with a new reality. There is also the great regret that I never got to share so much more about his life and family history and that's one reason why I am happy to fill in some of the gaps with this book.

It was a deeply unsettling time and I probably found hard, unrelenting physical work was as good a way to escape things as anything. Fortunately for me, I had my wonderful Jeep to take me anywhere I wanted to go. Unfortunately for me, it took me to a lovely boozy evening in Nottingham with some older friends at the Yates's Wine lodge where I had an awful lot of Australian port. Well, it always seems a good idea at the time, doesn't it?

Now forgive me if you already know this but the Yates's Wine Lodges are Britain's oldest pub chain set up in 1884 in Oldham by Peter and Simon Yates. Their motto was "moderation is the true temperance" by which they meant that the good citizens of Britain should forgo the wickedness and debauchery brought on by gin drinking and turn instead to the healthy, less destructive alternative of wine – or in my case the deadly Australian port. I can't escape the irony.

So, after emptying a vineyard or two, I was off home. In those days there wasn't much traffic on the road, and I was merrily scudding along in my sturdy Jeep back towards Newark when I came across a large traffic island. Clearly, there was something fundamentally wrong with this piece of road furniture as I found myself heading rather speedily around the edge of this obstruction, taking out some of the Keep Left signs on the way round and ending up in a ditch, in close proximity to a telegraph pole.

Now I'm not trying to excuse my behaviour, but it did seem a little unlucky that in double quick time, a police car happened by and understandably stopped to find out what had happened. Initially, they said they would look for the driver, not thinking it could be young me, but I had to confess in the end, and I was off to the police station. It was what you might call a sobering experience.

Now those were days when everyone knew everyone and once they had charged me, the police called my mother and explained that I had partaken of more than a thimble full of strong liquor and would she like them to bring me home. Full credit to my mother she replied in no uncertain terms: "Certainly not, a night in the cells will do him good." So that was that and I ended up spending my only night ever in a police cell. It's not something I would recommend, and it ended with me getting banned from driving which was a bit of a nuisance as I was shortly to pack my bags for Cirencester and the next undistinguished stage of my education.

It also led to one of the few negative headlines I have ever generated in the local press: "Australian port led to court". On the plus side, I am eternally indebted to my wonderful mother who though she was pretty unimpressed with my behaviour, started driving me to all my jobs. Throughout the months before I left for college, she tirelessly supported me, pulling my machines along behind us on the trailer. I didn't need reminding that if it hadn't been for her, my early business career would have been over. And stay away from Australian port.

There was one other blow to my hopes. At this stage it was not clear what the state of my father's estate would be. Throughout my early years, as I have said, I had always thought I would become a farmer. My ever-generous father was happy to invest in a farm which I would be able to run as his proxy. As it would transpire after I had finished at Cirencester, his premature death meant that dream died with him, but I had, at that time no idea and still thought farming would be my life. With the benefit of many years of hindsight, I'm so relieved I didn't end up in agriculture as I have several friends for whom it is a permanent struggle to make ends meet.

But it was to severely limit my options going forward. Since my father's estate was frozen, there could be no farm for me to run, no fields for me to plough, no tractors for me to drive. But I am once again getting ahead of myself. For now, there was one vital piece of my education to complete – the Cirencester Agricultural College of Drinking and Misbehaviour. I would thoroughly recommend it as long as you don't expect actually to learn anything. Beware Cirencester, Charles is on his way.

Chapter Three

*

Make friends – they will help you

These days if you ever want to visit what is now rather grandly called the Royal Agricultural University, Cirencester, you can take a virtual tour on-line. In my time there in the late fifties, you still had to enter through the somewhat imposing Victorian-Gothic front door into the wood panelled hall. It's all very grand and quite impressive in its lovely Cotswold stone exterior. But for me, a lot of it proved a waste of time.

If you look up the history of what was then the Royal Agricultural College – it was given university status in 2003 – it's not just the buildings which seemed quite impressive. Founded in 1842 by the Fairford and Cirencester Farmers' Club, it first opened its doors to 25 students in 1845 under the patronage of Queen Victoria, no less. It's had royal patrons ever since.

The problem for me is best illustrated in the college

motto, which I believe is taken from Virgil's Georgics and goes 'Avorum Cultus Pecorumque'. Now I'm not going to pretend that I will translate that myself but in plain English it means "Caring for the fields and the beasts" and that's my problem. I didn't care for either the fields or the beasts, I just wanted to drive a tractor and that wasn't on the curriculum.

Now I have already openly said, I don't have much of an academic bent and the year I spent at Cirencester just made me realise that my future lay in something far more down to earth and practical. The place was stuffed with former admirals, captains and a fair smattering of Right Honourables who were in training to run the family estates and huge farms. The truth is it taught me a lot about how to relate to these highly educated, older people. It was nothing as formal as etiquette, I already knew which knife and fork to use. It was about understanding and interaction; the fundamental ways in which people connect and how we get along. Though I say it myself, I was getting pretty good at getting along with people. That's why I have called this chapter 'Make friends, they will help you'.

Now, for any of you budding entrepreneurs out there, this simple maxim may strike you as a statement of the bloody obvious. Well, may I say, I agree with you but there is also a good reason why clichés are what they are. Just because something has been said over and over again doesn't invalidate it. Quite the reverse I might say. So get out there and make a few friends, a thought which would lead me naturally to the trade fairs in Cologne. But now I really do get ahead of myself. More of that anon.

The truth is, the Cirencester bunch were a pleasant

enough crowd and I got on pretty well with most of them, though I only have one close friend from that period with whom I am still in touch and that's the redoubtable Labrador breeder David Smith. He has much the same, rather blurred, recollection of our time at Cirencester though he claims to have done a bit more work than me. However, it was a beautiful area with a good collection of excellent pubs so we could at least make merry. Hence the blurred memory.

We lodged in a rather lovely stone-faced house near the centre of town which was run by a rather less lovely stone-faced woman who was a former senior member of the armed forces – I think she may have been a brigadier. She certainly behaved like one. We weren't allowed any visitors and she kept us four lads pretty much in check. We got breakfast and a three-course traditional dinner which left us free to take our lunch at the wonderful King's Head in Market Place. That became our unofficial headquarters. What's more, I fell madly in love with the manageress of WH Smith. She was called Valentine and although she was ten years older than me, I was smitten, and she certainly taught me a thing or two, but I had better draw a discreet veil over that.

Though I'm not trying to re-write the Good Pub Guide, I have to put in some words of praise for the King's Head. There has been a coaching inn on the site since the fourteenth century and for most of its existence it belonged to the Strange family. Rather like my parents' hotel in Newark, it had its own small place in history when in 1642 a certain Lord Chandos pitched up to try and recruit soldiers for Charles 1st to fight in the civil war. Well, it seems the town was violently parliamentarian and the locals set out to get him. Luckily for his Lordship, he found refuge in the King's Head. I can only hope that, like me, he appreciated the excellent cask ales.

You know, I can still picture walking in the front door, past the posh cocktail bar on the left and into the back where you could get a pint and a meal. It was good old fashioned pub fayre of sausage and chips and no doubt, a jar of pickled eggs on the bar. It was a great place to be and there were some really friendly local people whose company I enjoyed, though I vividly remember one night when I came badly unstuck, and which has given a lifelong aversion to whisky.

Back in the late fifties, there was a television series called Lockhart of the Yard which starred an actor called Raymond Francis. Well, I assume he was filming somewhere in the area and that's why he was staying at the King's Head. He was a lovely chap and we got talking but since he was a whisky drinker, I felt obliged to join him. What I remember most about the evening was that I got alcohol poisoning and spent most of the next few days in bed recovering. As I say, I haven't been able to touch the stuff since.

But the atmosphere at the college was always pretty relaxed. Because I wasn't remotely interested in cattle, I didn't bother attending those lectures, but I did go to the ones to do with crops because I still thought my future lay in farming. A lot of the stuff we did was outdoors, and we would pile into a hired bus and go off and see some practical demonstrations of good farming practice – most of which I found genuinely interesting and informative.

My mate David recalls a fair amount of practical tuition outdoors – the university now runs three farms of its own

– but I don't think the young Charles Lawrence was fully engaged. Upon reflection, I'm not saying that year was a complete waste of time because it was not only fun, but it also helped to shape me for the future. From the people I met at college to the dozens or maybe hundreds of associates I have come to meet through business, I have always tried to get on with people and as I have said, that has paid dividends in every area of my working life.

There was a bit of crackpot behaviour when I was at college. For instance, a bunch of the Cirencester lads (not me) went off and painted some yellow ducks on the Vulcan bombers at nearby South Cerney airfield which is now known as the Duke of Gloucester's Barracks. It caused a bit of a stir at the time because the son of someone rather prominent was involved, though it's just as well, given the ease of access, they weren't enemy spies. However, I did get involved with transport when we planted a windsock on the tower of the college. Just high spirits, indeed spirits were almost certainly involved.

There was also the time when the man who would go on to be president of the National Farmers Union, one Sir David Naish, offered me a lift home because he lived near Newark. He drove me nearly all the way home then said he was turning off the road and dumped me by the roadside. I was standing by the side of the Fosse Way feeling a total prat with my suitcase in my hand and my thumb out hitchhiking when a mate of mine pulled over. Luckily, once he'd finished laughing at me, he gave me a lift.

Now I have never been much of a Round Table "you scratch my back and I'll scratch yours" type of chap. It's more that if you are approachable and open, people are going to be far more likely to trust you and want to do business with you. Equally, there have been times when I have walked away from what could have been very big bits of business because, quite frankly, I looked across the table at the people on the other side and I thought, "I'm not having anything to do with you. Goodbye."

Now that may have cost me some money, but it has never cost me a sleepless night because I knew with absolute certainty that it was the right thing to do. And let me tell you, I've seen some pretty astonished expressions on the faces opposite me when I have gathered up my papers, clipped shut my briefcase and headed out of the door. It certainly felt good though.

Neuroscientists reckon that it takes someone roughly seven seconds to decide whether or not you like people when you meet them for the first time. Now, friends have been kind enough to tell me over the years that I am an excellent judge of character and when I think of the many folk I have had the privilege and pleasure to work with, I am inclined to think my friends are probably right.

And by that, I don't just mean the great and good with whom I have done business. I mean the excellent folk on the shop floor and in the factory who have so often reinforced my faith in them. Everyone knows me by my first name, and everyone has known that I was always approachable and would try to find time to listen to a problem or a grievance.

Anyone who knows me will also tell you that in all my early business ventures, the suit I was most likely to be seen in was a boiler suit and I have certainly never feared getting my hands greasy. At the same time, in business you have to know when it's time to slip the silk hankie into the breast pocket of a three-piece suit and look like the boss.

So like I say, what my year at Cirencester taught me was far more about what I didn't want to do and that, in its own way, helped push me in the direction of where I did want to go. It took another couple of years' back-breaking work on a farm before it all finally started to come together in business and personal terms. But you must see life as a journey not an event. And you also have to have some fun. I certainly have done, but more of that too, later in the book.

Me as a teenager

At Cirencester with friends: Chris Graham, Johnny Banks and Richard Dale 1960

A lot of the time it had all been a laugh but there was a growing sense of unease in me. I won't say it was raging ambition but at that time, once I had left Cirencester, I was still doing my rotavator business and earning more from doing someone's garden than for a full day's graft on the farm. I just couldn't escape the idea that I would have to make the jump and start working full time for myself.

It wasn't that I had a clear strategy or business model, but something was gnawing at me and I had to listen to my inner voice. All my business life I have always jumped at the next chance and tried to take advantage of it. It wasn't like I had a master plan, but I guess I am a restless soul who can't just stand still. Well, I was about to make the first leap along a road to what would become the Charles Lawrence Group. Though if you'd told me that at the time, I'd have told you not to be so daft and get me a pint.

It was tough on my mother to begin with because, like I've explained, I still hadn't got my driving licence back, so she had to drive me and the machinery to any jobs I was doing. It's a great tribute to the evenness of her disposition that she never complained but drove me to the locations day after day until I finally got my licence back. My farm-buying plans were permanently on hold due to the continued freezing of my father's estate. However with the £1,000 I had been allowed to inherit, I invested in a Morris Minor Traveller – another British motoring classic with its wooden beams at the back.

I can't resist filling you in with a bit of history because the Morris Minor was designed by Alex Issigonis, the father of the Mini, and launched at the Earls Court Motor show in September 1948. Altogether, the Morris Minor sold more than 1.6 million vehicles and only stopped production in 1972. It was the first design ever to sell more than a million examples and I loved it – though I still had my heart set on my Rolls Royce by the age of 30. It was a slow beginning, but the work gradually started to increase, and I was about to embark on the first – and probably hairiest – period of business expansion. Time to take a deep breath, it wasn't all plain sailing.

Chapter Four

*

Never over promise, always deliver

Have I ever mentioned that I love driving tractors? Okay, just checking that you've been paying attention because I was about to build a landscaping business which should have been my idea of tractor-driving heaven. Sadly, I was going to be far too busy to do much of the driving myself and had to employ a whole bunch of people to do the work for me – starting with the admirable Jimmy Dunn. I often wonder what happened to him after he left my employ, and I can only hope he didn't just drink himself to an early grave.

Now I'm a great believer in acknowledging help and kindness when you are given it. So here I must thank one of the main influences on my early business life – Mr Ted Hornsby. He was rather grandly titled the Depot Superintendent with the Ministry of Public Buildings and Works. But even that grandiloquent job title doesn't pay due reverence to the huge impact he could have, and how much control he exercised over the local area. You've got to remember that things were done so differently then and, like the bank manager who had a huge degree of autonomy over who got a loan, Mr Hornsby handed out the contracts. His word was law.

At the same time, in a cash-driven, low technology, poor supervision economy let me just say that questionable business practices were very common – and the depot superintendent was no exception. It was the way things were done in the sixties and while I was no Del Boy Trotter endlessly looking for a scam, Mr Hornsby did make it clear that if I wanted the business then we did it his way or it really was the highway. So his way it was.

It all started when I was contacted to do some rotavating at Mr Hornsby's place and duly turned up to do his garden. I can still picture him today in his suit and tie and his balding head. He was a classic gruff northern businessman who had run a construction company of his own, but I think it must have gone bust. But he was also quite an imposing person to meet, and he commanded a lot of respect and, in return, was very respectful to the senior figures he was dealing with though they all called him Ted. He knew his way around and could swear like a trooper. His wife was lovely – a real Scunthorpe sort of person who was stout but sophisticatedly stout, if you get my drift.

All I can say is that he must have taken a shine to me. Let's face it, Newark was, and is, quite a small community so once you were known as honest and reliable, it wasn't hard to find the work. So, it was Mr Hornsby who suggested to me that I should get my name on the approved list of contractors for the public sector, and I said honestly that I hadn't a clue how to go about it. So he did it for me. Suddenly, I was getting all sorts of local authority contracts to cut grass at everything from sports fields to aerodromes.

There was even a weird one when Mr Hornsby asked if I knew there was a tender going for someone to manage a dump for a number of local RAF stations. Well to be honest, if it hadn't been for him I don't think I would ever have heard about it, but he was also very encouraging. You have to bear in mind that at that time in the sixties, the UK was downsizing everywhere overseas with colonies getting their independence and no involvement 'East of Suez' following the Suez crisis in 1956. That meant a lot of stuff from the Naafi was simply being dumped as everything was scaled back. I should explain that the Navy, Army and Air Force Institute (Naafi) was founded in 1920 to provide services to military personnel.

Thanks to Mr Hornsby, I got the contract and went out and bought a bulldozer to manage the waste. It was a second hand International BTD6 with a four in one bucket which I bought from R. Cripps in Lower Parliament Street, Nottingham. Isn't it odd what you can remember when you put your mind to it? You can still buy International bulldozers for a few thousand pounds on eBay, though it seems Cripps disappeared in the mid-sixties – certainly it closed the Nottingham premises then.

But there is another aspect of this which might shed some light on my character and my need for thrift. When the Naafi was cleaning out its unwanted stuff, among the clothing they threw out was a rather handsome three-piece brown suit. Well I couldn't let a good piece of tailoring go to waste. I am happy to say that the suit was saved, fitted me perfectly and had a long and happy life about my person, much to the amusement of my friends.

You may laugh, but I was always cautious about money at that stage. Even today, I still get friends and family asking me why I don't just go out and spend more. At that time, I barely paid myself anything and was always careful to make sure I had enough ready money to pay the workforce; there were times when I thought nothing of carrying around two grand in cash. How quickly the workforce spent their wages, was none of my business. You've got to bear in mind that when I was building my business, there was no question of crowd funding or peer to peer lending, you had to generate your own cash flow and get a little help from the bank manager. The manager of my local Barclays was Mr Tanner and luckily for me, he knew I came from a respectable family and I could be trusted.

Through Mr Tanner's good offices, I got an overdraft of £2,500 which allowed me to pay the workers promptly until my invoices were settled. The quid pro quo was that I had to go and see Mr Tanner once a month and give him a run-down of my finances and how the business was going. In good time, he increased the overdraft facility to £5000 but in the meantime, I had to get stuck in and generate the income. Even in those days back in the sixties, I was making good profits but as soon as I got my hand on any money, I would go and get another machine for the business.

Look, I'm not saying I was some kind of business genius, but I know I had several things going in my favour. The people I worked for seemed to like me and certainly trusted me; I worked hard and never tried to over-charge or over-promise. As far as I remember, I met my first employee – dear old Jimmy – in the pub and offered him £2 a day plus a bottle of milk. Within a matter of years, I had thirty blokes, all of them Irish, on my payroll. But more of that later.

It seems to me I should fill you in with a bit of the economic background. Maybe the sixties didn't exactly swing for me, but in business terms they were certainly moving in a sharply upwards trajectory. There was a load of post-war rebuilding going on and huge demand for new housing. Wimpey was one of my first big clients and there was hardly anyone else in the area around Newark doing the same as me – landscaping, planting and grass cutting. I'm not saying it was glamorous, but it was certainly lucrative. Sometimes very lucrative. It's funny now when I'm driving around the Newark area I will regularly turn to Vanessa and say, "I planted that."

Generally, the sixties were a benign time for business. Although under the government of Harold Wilson taxes were high, the economy was growing steadily despite a high pound. If you look at the economic growth figures from the end of 1959 to 1970 there was continual expansion, as measured by Gross Domestic Product, in every single quarter.

Rising living standards meant increasing purchases of white goods – fridges, washing machines and the like – as well as cars. There was a big shift from public transport, aided by Dr Beeching's cuts to the rail network, to private cars. Car ownership went from 40 to 60 per cent of the population, though maybe not everyone was as keen on car ownership as I was.

What's more house ownership was still very affordable. Even in 1969 the average house price in England and Wales was £4,328. In the late fifties and sixties, a million new homes were built – many of them for social housing and Charles Lawrence Landscapes was there to provide ancillary services in the gardening industry. With hindsight, it was all a bit crazy but with the right contacts and the correct work ethic, I just got busier and busier.

You see on the one hand, there were decent – if slightly questionable – people like Mr Hornsby who had a huge amount of power and influence over the award of contracts. On the other hand, they simply wanted people they could rely on to deliver those contracts with no fuss or trouble. That's what I did. My point is that although there was no elaborate tendering process, if you proved you were diligent and could deliver what you had promised, then you were fast tracked for other contracts.

Let me give you a somewhat random example. We had a big government food store in Newark, presumably to avoid shortages, called the Buffer Depot. It really only amounted to row upon row of Nissen huts full of sugar and other vital food stocks. I won the contract to cut the grass around the huts. No big deal but the workload was constantly growing. Mind you, on the downside it meant no holidays or luxuries for me. It could also be extremely stressful if things didn't go the way they were planned – but I never ever thought of giving up.

It might all seem a bit odd to young people, but the way I did business then was something like this: I had five or six Land Rovers which would be waiting at the bus station in Newark first thing in the morning to deliver the workers to their jobs. Pay was £2 a day plus a bottle of milk and the rules were pretty simple: do a good day's work and you can come back tomorrow, mess things up and you can look elsewhere for work. My mate Geoffrey says he can remember watching me pay out the wages on a Friday evening, only to have some of them coming to ask for a loan on Monday because they'd squandered the lot on a weekend of heavy drinking. But for the most part I have to say they were as good as gold.

Me on my first tractor – a David Brown Cropmaster – in my twenties

Naturally, there were exceptions. I got a contract to cut the grass along the road from Wolverhampton to Stone. It was a big ministerial contract and I had to import the first

With my friends Johnny Banks, Geoffrey Bond, Tony Masding and Pat Burke
circa 1965

flail mower from the United States. They're as common as muck these days, but then to have a heavy-duty mower on a hydraulic arm so you could cut grass on the banks was a real novelty. So I bought Jimmy Dunn a scruffy old caravan and told him to get on with it. Unfortunately, if I turned up on a Monday morning, the caravan would be deserted and the mower unused because Jimmy had been on the lash over the weekend.

But I was also very methodical and kept records on everything. I even have my very first invoice for laying a lawn – I think I got £1.50 – and I have my very first set of accounts from 1964. Though as I have freely admitted I never had a master plan, I did try and keep track of everything that was going on. No-one has ever accused me of being a micro-manager (well not to my face at least) but I have always embraced every challenge with an open mind.

Equally, everyone is allowed to fail from time to time. I'd have to admit that not everything I have had a go at was a shining triumph. But it's one of the vital aspects of success in business that you have to be allowed to fail sometimes. Even more important though is that you learn something from that failure, understand what you did badly and ensure you don't do it again. Luckily for me, I was so busy at that stage that even if something did go a bit wrong, I had so many other issues to preoccupy me that there was no time to sob into my pillow. It was "hi ho, hi ho…" as Snow White's chums would have said.

And that's maybe how I got into the demolition business. As I have said, there was still a great deal of post-war development going on in the late sixties and early seventies and the old back-to-back housing was on its way out so multi-storey blocks of flats could take their place. Now, I will leave it to you to judge whether that was progress or not. But I did get a large contract to demolish an area of Nottingham known as the Meadows.

The area had become pretty run down and many of the terraced houses which were built in the 19th century for railway and factory workers were considered no longer fit for purpose. Now the secret of quick demolition of whole streets is that you take the roof off all the houses in the row, use a hydraulic excavator to bash down the chimney at one end and then there is a domino effect as one chimney stack knocks the next one over.

It only took a couple of minutes for the whole lot to come down. But there is one other essential part of the process and that is to demolish entirely the house on the end where you want the domino effect to stop. On one memorable occasion, what my guys had failed to do, was to take out the house next to the corner shop at the end of the row. Unfortunately, the demolition domino did its work extremely effectively but also took out a large chunk of the corner shop which had people in it. Fortunately, no one was hurt. Well, maybe my pride was a bit dented, but I survived.

You know, it's a funny thing when you start raking over old memories because rather like buses, one comes along, followed almost immediately by another. Your brain is like a warehouse full of dusty old files. By the time you get to my age and start remembering, it's like sending the old janitor off through the warehouse to get the files and he struggles back with his sack truck loaded with stuff and he's brought the file you wanted but he's picked up a load of other stuff as well. Thanks to an article in the Newark Advertiser (some of which is accurate) another file has just arrived. Here's the story.

Bearing in mind that I knew nothing about demolition other than asking myself, "Well how hard can it actually be to knock something down?" I got another big job to demolish an old mill in the lovely Yorkshire town of Richmond. It's a gorgeous place on the edge of the Yorkshire Dales with a lovely Norman castle in the middle and I happily trundled off there with the gear on a low loader for what should have been a routine job. Well, it was anything but.

At the end of the old mill was a small cottage, presumably the old mill owner's residence. All of a sudden, a chap comes out of the cottage with a shotgun pointing right at me. "You're not going to knock down my cottage," he stated defiantly. Now, if I have one maxim which has always stood me in good stead, it's that if you are yourself unarmed, then the person with the gun is always right. I'd love to say that I stood up to him in a manly way and told him to put his firearm down. Instead, I nearly wet myself and said rather lamely, "Look mate I'm only here to do my job."

Well, I'm relieved to say he did calm down and agreed to leave the cottage so I could get on with my highly skilled and professional approach to demolition. After a bit of thought, it occurred to me that the best and easiest way to get rid of an old wooden mill in such a remote location was to burn it down. So I torched it and within no time at all, there was nothing but some smouldering embers and a bit of tangled old machinery. A word of advice – don't go trying the same trick today.

However, the job was by no means completed as the second part of my task was to level a couple of acres of ground running down to the River Swale and turf the lot as a picnic area for the locals. We did a lovely job, and I was genuinely proud of the beautiful setting we were going to leave behind as a new local amenity. Even better, the necessary officials came out and applauded our work so we would get paid for everything.

What we could not have factored in, was the weather. Anyone who knows that area will tell you that the River Swale is one of the fastest rising waterways in England. Not only was it always prone to flooding, but the situation was made even worse by decades of lead mining which had stripped the soil bare and left lots of channels carved out for the industry to speed the flow of water. I imagine you can work out for yourself what happened next.

Indeed, just a couple of days after proudly laying our two thousand square meters of turf, the skies darkened, and torrential rains washed the whole lot down the river. From there, some of it would have been swept into the River Ure and then it was only a hop, skip and a flood to the River Ouse.

Get that look off your face, I might have had some pretty powerful contacts even at that stage of my life – but they weren't that powerful. Sadly, I didn't have a celestial contact on speed dial. So there was nothing for it but to go back and put the whole lot down for a second time. I'm relieved to say that, as far as I know, it's all still there today and has withstood many a subsequent flood.

Now, I have to say with hindsight, it felt like a dream sequence. Remember I am a young man in my early twenties with no vast fortune to fall back on. I am now managing a raft of contracts for grass cutting and landscaping for the local authorities, the RAF and their airfields as well as huge private sector companies like Wimpey who were building loads of houses and flats in the area. I was, in essence, the ring master for a growing circus of performers or maybe a better analogy is that I was keeping an awful lot of plates spinning on poles without really knowing what might happen next.

That was about the time I got the contract to landscape the whole of the 35 acres of grounds at Nottingham University. It was a huge job to get it looking as good as it still does today, and that bulldozer certainly came in very handy. Nottingham moved to University Park in 1928 after a benefactor gave them the land and it got its royal charter and became the University of Nottingham in 1948. I kept the maintenance contract until the surveyor retired but by then my eyes were already looking for a fresh business opportunity. Things were about to get a lot more interesting

On a personal note, I had got married in 1969 to a lovely

young woman called Valerie Hyde who used to ride past my mother's house on horseback. We got hitched when she was in her late teens and I was in my mid-twenties and lived in a lovely house in Lincolnshire which I bought for four and a half thousand pounds and which I noticed sold recently for a quarter of a million. Despite having two adorable baby girls (more about them in the chapter on family) sadly, it didn't work out. We got divorced six years later but we remain on friendly terms and she now lives back in Newark.

For the record, I did get my first Rolls Royce before I reached thirty. Cars really were my only luxury, and I did get a kick of going down to the pub in my bottle green Silver Cloud 3. In the early days, my friends used to take the mickey when I turned up for a pint in my old boiler suit and they'd be ribbing me saying, "Got the rotavator on your trailer, Charles?" Well, they didn't laugh quite so loudly once I pitched up in the Roller.

But like I said, I really didn't squander money on luxuries and when I submitted my first audited accounts, I think there was a profit of about a thousand pounds. It wasn't really until the end of the sixties, start of the seventies that I began to pay myself a proper salary. I was still working flat out and to be honest, once the business got a lot bigger I did have the occasional sleepless night wondering how I was going to pay the bills. Frankly, it was far more serious than that, but this is yet another issue I will return to, later in this narrative.

The advantage was, in those days, most people were very prompt in settling invoices and, in return, I was very quick to pay anything which I owed. It's a habit I have maintained throughout my business career and even today if I need something done, local tradespeople always know they'll get their money as soon as they bill me. I keep reminding them that the job isn't over until you've been paid. Sadly, paying promptly is not always the case in today's business world. But I guess I'm just a bit old fashioned and proud of it. It certainly didn't hurt my reputation as I moved into the next and more interesting part of my business career. Goodbye grass seeds, hello synthetic surfaces.

Chapter Five

*

Embrace change

There are several sepia-tinged photographs from the early seventies which always make me smile and maybe feel a bit nostalgic about the fun we had in the early days in the synthetic surfaces business. They feature me and my nephew Nigel, stripped to the waist and looking like a couple of roadies for a rock band or a pair of hippies too stoned to know the sixties had ended. Together, we were a kind of lash-up, somewhere between Laurel and Hardy and Don Quixote and Sancho Panza. But we did a bloody good job.

In fact, we were laying some of the first polyurethane tennis court surfaces in France; though it was undoubtedly hard work, we had a great time doing it. Nigel is 17 years younger than me and was still at the University of Nottingham studying for his degree in surveying so I used to save up the French jobs so we could do them in the holidays. One of the photos clearly shows my Volkswagen van emblazoned with the words Elastosol, the trademark for the surface, and Porous Synthetic Surfaces written in English and French.

Since I still had to run the increasingly busy UK end of the business during the week, Nigel and I would pack up the sacks of rubber granules and the coloured polyurethane and, on a Friday afternoon, belt off to catch the ferry from Newhaven. There was endless faffing around with what the customs people called carnets – the documents you needed to get things out of the country without paying duty. In the days before the EU, you had to persuade them that you were taking the stuff out to do a demonstration and you would be bringing it all back. Well, it didn't actually come back but they would take one look at the filthy polyurethane coated containers in the back of the van on the return journey and they didn't need much persuading not to check.

Nigel and I still laugh about those days, partly because we must have looked a fright after spraying the tennis courts with the polyurethane. We found that not only did it stick to our hands, clothing and hair, but there was no way you could wash it off. It was like having a permanent pair of rubber gloves and you had to wear them off. I remember doing a hotel tennis court in France and, by the end, we were in such a state, they wouldn't let us eat in the hotel restaurant and we had to take our food in the kitchen.

However, this does go to the heart of my business philosophy. I did the dirty, back-breaking work myself because it had to be done properly and I knew exactly how it should be done. Going forwards, I would always show a new employee the right way to do things and they always knew that I could, and would, do the job myself. I would never ask anyone to do a job that I would not do myself and if that meant standing looking like an escapee from the local clowns' school, then so be it. Vanity never did feature very high on my list of early priorities. It still doesn't.

The other aspect of my approach which is desperately important, is that if you were doing business with me, you didn't just buy a product or a service – you got me, and my reputation thrown in. Now that meant that if something went wrong, then I was there to fix it. That wasn't merely an empty promise, it was from my heart. Later on I will tell you how, on a single project, it would cost me a quarter of a million quid to put it right. While that still stings a bit, it is important you understand that about me and who I am.

Back to the French stuff and I'm not even sure we made much money out of it, but I had been introduced to the former chairman of ICI France, Arthur Reincke, who lived in Paris and enjoyed the good things in life – actually he enjoyed the best things in life and I rather enjoyed sharing them with him. The connection had come through Geoffrey Bond who had been staying in a lovely place called the Hotel Mome in Cavaliere in the south of France. Like me, Geoffrey is a chatty sort of guy and he got talking to the old Etonian and fellow Brit, Mr Reincke. That's how we got our first contact with ICI and I will explain later just where it all led.

Now to this generation, the name of Imperial Chemical Industries might merely produce a bemused shrug. Who? Well, I'll have you know that ICI was once the biggest manufacturer in Britain having been formed in 1926 with the merger of four leading British chemicals companies. Run from its impressive headquarters on the banks of the Thames near Westminster, ICI made everything from Dulux paints and speciality polymers to electronic components, fragrances and food flavourings.

At its height, it was a considered a bellwether for the state of the British economy. Incidentally, in case you don't know, the word bellwether came from the shepherd's practice of putting a bell around the neck of a castrated ram (a wether) so he could hear where the flock was even when it was out of sight. Now I bet you didn't know that did you? Well, nor did I until I looked it up.

However, the ICI story is also a classic tale of how British industry went into decline from the end of the Second World War to the present day, when services account for more than two thirds of the British economy. ICI was acquired in 2008 by the Dutch company AkzoNobel, bits of it were sold off and the rest integrated into its new owner. The HQ was also flogged off though the building still stands proudly next to MI5's headquarters on Millbank.

Anyway, back to France where Nigel and I would drive hundreds of miles to do a tennis court and then belt back again to the UK. We covered courts from Chantilly and Versailles to Jenzat in central France and St Nazaire. Nigel has reminded me about one weekend when a bloke in the south of France, who had been our agent in the area, decided to pack it in. So, we got in my car – a rather smart Rover SDI – and drove south, took the machine he had to pieces, put them all in the car, had lunch with him and started the long drive back. When we were getting near to the ferry at Dieppe, it was obvious we were just going to miss it. Instead, we had a good French dinner and then drove to the port and slept in the car until we could get the next sailing which was the following day. Then it was straight back to work. Bonkers, but great fun.

On the other hand, there were times when we could relax. When we went to the job in Versailles, we had to wait for a few days for the materials to arrive. We found a good bar in a sunny spot and sat it out as best we could, watching the people go by. And I certainly won't let Nigel forget the time we were on a two-lane road, heading for Rouen in the dead of night, when I suddenly noticed a car behind us being driven erratically and at high speed. As he passed us, he clipped the side of the van. So to set our nerves at rest, I pulled over into a small layby. There was no real damage done and we were about to set off again when I noticed someone had dumped a load of cardboard sheets in the woods. "Come on Nigel," I said, "Let's get these in the van." He thought I was off my head, but I wanted them to protect the sides of the tennis courts when we were spraying them. Now that's what I call thrifty.

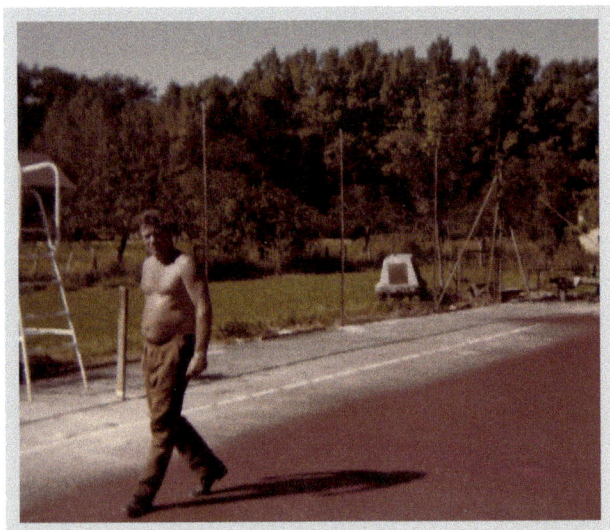

Working on an Elastosol surface in Jenzat, France early eighties

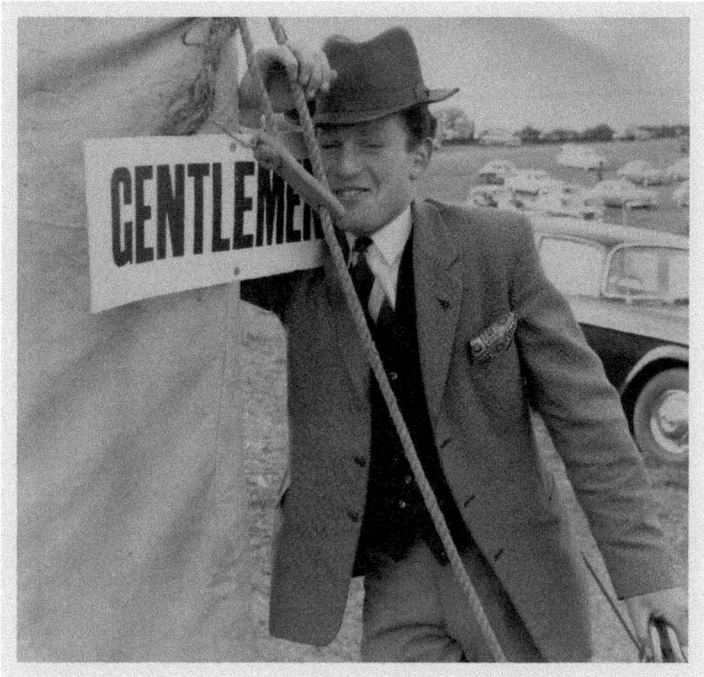

Enjoying the Newark and Nottinghamshire County Show circa 1964

Now would be a good time to introduce you to the other key figure who made my start in artificial surfaces a reality. As I mentioned earlier, Geoffrey had met Mr Reincke and put us in touch with ICI but even more crucially, he in turn introduced us to the German artificial surfaces contractor and manufacturer Horst Willnow. It transpired that at that time, Horst was the biggest purchaser of rubber granules from ICI anywhere in Europe. What's more, in his factory in Ulm in the south of Germany, he was also making the machines to spread the granules and resurface tennis courts and children's playgrounds.

On my first trip to Hamburg to meet Horst, I was accompanied by a local Davis cup tennis champion, Tony Pickard, whose family had a building business in the Nottingham area. Now Tony had a distinguished playing and coaching career in tennis, though he's probably best known for his long association with the former world number one Stefan Edberg. Mind you, he also captained the Davis Cup team led by Tim Henman and he coached Greg Rusedski for a while. Well, he came along with me to give his professional opinion on the quality of the new surface.

Although Horst wasn't everyone's cup of Jagermeister, we hit it off famously from the start. He was a short guy with a balding grey head and a bit of a pot belly, but his English was completely fluent, and he spoke it almost without an accent. He'd started his career playing drums in a Hamburg strip club but by the time I met him, he was selling rubber and the machines necessary to turn it into sports surfaces around the world.

There are some great videos online – originally shot in 35mm black and white as well as technicolour film – of Hamburg in the seventies. They bring back so many memories of a city which had completely shaken off its post war blues and was thriving. There are scenes of crowded streets and very short skirts, modern restaurants and new shopping centres. The German economy was booming, though it's still funny to see in the pictures, the older generation very much in shirt and tie and the youngsters with defiantly long hair and whiskers. Hamburg has a pretty racy reputation even today and trust me, it is well deserved.

Now, as for my man Horst, his great strength was that he understood the chemistry of the nascent industry in which we were working. Though I remained very fond of him, to be honest, his great weakness was that if he made a Deutschmark, he would spend rather more than a Deutschmark. Again, for my younger readers, I should explain that the DM preceded the Euro as the German national currency.

He also had the great good fortune of being married to the glorious Ankee, who could drink her own weight in single malt whiskey and was fantastic fun to have around. I can't deny that we did have a few differences of opinion during the years we collaborated. But it's a sign of the strength of our underlying relationship that he called us every Christmas Day until he died in 2019. Sadly, I wasn't well enough to go to his funeral but of Horst, I have many fond memories.

Back at home in Newark, the business was still just me, Nigel and a part time secretary – with some large bags of rubber granules and a machine for spraying the surfaces. I do remember I had to source a mixer from the United States. It was no good trying to use a concrete mixer for rubber and polyurethane because some of it would get stuck around the edge. So I bought an Essex plaster mixer which meant that the blades would thoroughly wipe the edges and ensure that everything was properly mixed together.

It was all pretty basic science. It was like having a toothpaste tube packed with the mixture and we would simply spray it out. Having said that, the very first tennis court took us ages whereas now, you could do two courts in a day and they would be cured and ready to use within a few hours, if the weather was right. What's more, I can honestly say we were the pioneers in lots of aspects of this emerging technology and though the transition from landscaping and lawns was painful, even traumatic, we weathered some serious financial challenges and came through. Let's just say we learned some difficult lessons on the way.

Generally, the business started a period of steady growth through the eighties and nineties. Like most people, I have 20-20 hindsight and could claim it was a well-planned trajectory from those early days to what became the Charles Lawrence Group. In fact, it was a seat of the pants, breathless roller coaster of a transition where we came close to extinction a few times. And, as I will tell you later, on a couple of occasions things went horribly wrong. Though I will also tell you what we did to put it all right.

It was probably just a mixture of my stubborn pride and sheer cussedness, Nigel's attention to detail, Horst Willnow's technology and support from good friends and business partners like Geoffrey Bond which made it all happen. But none of it was planned in a strategic fashion. It's the very essence of being a successful entrepreneur that you have to be flexible, fast and utterly determined. I was toying with the idea of saying ruthless, but I will let those who know me decide on that.

Speaking of Geoffrey, I was always a great fan of getting really good non-executive directors on the board. Alongside him were the equally estimable Ian Shaw – a senior partner at what was then the accountancy firm Touche Ross and Rob Carrol – a venture capitalist. Now I know I can be a *bit* difficult sometimes once I have got an idea in my head… okay I know I can be *bloody* difficult once I have got an idea in my head. However, I'm also the first to recognise that no one has a monopoly on good ideas and when you have people with the exceptional insight and ability of people like these around the board table then it pays to listen to them. Just as you should also listen to your workforce.

I'd even go so far as to make it a general principle of good leadership that you must never be afraid to surround yourself with people who are better and brighter than you are. If you don't mind, let's go back to Geoffrey. He's an extremely successful commercial lawyer who has had a hugely rewarding career in the City of London. To use the parallel of being allowed to drive your sheep across London Bridge as a freeman of the City – well Geoffrey would get the permits, Nigel would control the flock, but I was still the one who knew where they were going.

You know, I started with a photograph so let me finish this chapter with another one. I've already said that while I am not an overly ambitious person, I am certainly a competitive one. When I was young, I had that one big Rolls-Royce owning ambition which I achieved. This time, I can confess that by the time I'd reached 30, my new goal was to have an office block with my name on it in lights.

There is a rule of thumb for every industry that if you have your name on your shirt, you're probably not making much money: if you have your name on the office door, you are almost certainly doing alright and rising through the ranks: if you have your name on an office block in lights, you've pretty much made it.

So this time I won't keep you guessing. As I sit here in my study with the clock ticking in my ear, I am looking at a photograph of myself standing in front of an office block and there, behind me, is the sign saying Charles Lawrence. Like I have said, none of this was for the money but it was the desire to create and build something. When I look at that photograph, you will forgive me if I admit it does give me a sense of pride. From the wild boys with their flowing hair on the French tennis court to the man of business in front of an office block with my name on it. It was an extraordinary ten years and fortunately was only the beginning. Foreign countries were calling me, and I was only too happy to answer the call – even if they did often reverse the charges.

Chapter Six

*

Be adaptable

Now, when I think back over the last eighty years, it is true I never actually had a plan. Everything seemed to follow naturally from one project, one contract, one idea to the next. That's what makes entrepreneurs different from big business and big government. Totalitarian regimes have five-year plans then make up the numbers as they go along to ensure they meet their targets. Democratic regimes come up with shorter plans then largely ignore them.

Big business is the same. Driven by accountants and managers plotting Key Performance Indicators (KPIs) and Return on Investment (ROI), they can miss the opportunities which are staring them in the face. Well I didn't, because I was never hung up on some long-term goal but was always casting about for what I thought, and hoped, would make me a bob or two. Oh and I never let my ego get in the way, this was never just about me, it was about achieving something.

One of my old friends says it was really to make my late father Clifford proud of me. Well, maybe he's right, but I'll leave that to you and the shrinks to decide.

As I have said, the initial encounter with Mr Reincke had unearthed the information that artificial sports surfaces were a small but growing market and my friends knew me well enough to realise that this sort of thing was right up my boulevard. So we arranged to have a more formal meeting with Arthur Reincke in Paris. To be honest, even if nothing had ever come of it, neither of us needed much of an excuse to go and spend a few days in the French capital. There is always such a buzz about Paris and since both of us had a taste for good food and fine wine, it was the perfect place to do a bit of business and enjoy a lot of leisure. So that's what we did.

Having agreed we would work well together, one of the first people Mr Reincke put us in touch with was the head of research at an ICI laboratory in France. So Geoffrey and I went there to see what they had to offer. Geoffrey says he remembers the scene as clear as day when this chap opens his desk, takes out a five-inch square piece of material and gives it to me. It was a piece of Olymprene running track, the artificial surface trademarked by ICI. He says I bent it back and forward and then turned to him, "This is for us," I am alleged to have said. Well, it certainly turned out that it was!

Now I have been asked why I didn't just embrace the established technology – Olymprene – being offered by ICI. Well I can tell you that although I admired what they had done, I saw it as outdated technology. What I saw as the future in rain-soaked places like the UK was a porous track where the rain didn't pool on the surface allowing algae to develop.

Oh, and it was bloody expensive! Surfaces like Olymprene could end up as hard as concrete and though top athletes prefer a harder surface because they can achieve better times, the future for me was definitely porous. Not only could we provide a better product, but we could do it for two-thirds of the price.

Once I had got that clear understanding, the next, and much bigger step was to set up production. Fortunately we were already in touch with Horst Willnow in Hamburg, who had his own business making artificial tennis courts in Germany and, as I have said, was one of ICI's biggest buyers of polyurethane. We started buying our materials – including rubber granules – from Horst and we also set up our French limited liability company Charles Lawrence SARL. It was the birth of the international business and Mr Reincke became our representative in France.

Now the only slight issue was that by the time we had bought Arthur a car and paid his expenses for some rather elaborate entertaining in good restaurants, we didn't actually have much to show by way of profit. But this is where I would urge any budding entrepreneurs reading this to take the broader view. Ultimately, the connections which Arthur had through his association with ICI were invaluable and helped us build the network which would ultimately make the Charles Lawrence brand global. In the meantime, we did have a few very good meals.

Our very first tennis court was actually in the UK at Wollaton Village tennis club in 1974 and it was the very devil of a surface to lay. Horst had said we would have it done in a day and he did fly out to see how we got on, but after a couple of days he went back. It took Nigel and me a week of back-breaking labour to get the surface down. Frankly, the guys who were working with me on the landscaping and mowing weren't too keen on this sticky, smelly new technology. But we can honestly claim the country's first porous synthetic surface was eventually in place and now it was time to get serious.

We first set up the business on a one-acre plot next to where my house is now in Newark. We got all the materials and most of the equipment shipped from Germany. That rubber came from the peelings which were left when worn lorry tyres had their tread renewed. To repair them, they cut the tyre back to the underlying steel and then relayed the surface. Now that was easy enough because there was no steel in the mix. When we decided to recycle whole tyres with the steel inside them it proved far more challenging and indeed – explosive. But yet again, I'm getting ahead of myself.

While the expansion overseas was moving steadily, it was also full steam ahead at home. In particular, our Playtop brand of safe playground surfaces was growing steadily but was about to go stellar. One of the first ones we laid was a huge 600 square meter site in Portsmouth. Nigel and I had to put the whole surface down ourselves, working with trowels on our hands and knees. I remember we stayed in a nearby hotel for three days and at the end I turned to Nigel and said, "I'm stuffed if I am going to be doing this for the rest of my life." Well, I might have said something a bit fruitier than that.

Then in 1990, a BBC consumer affairs programme called 'That's Life' launched a campaign backed by the MP Paul Rose to prevent playground tragedies by installing safer playing surfaces. Now you can't stop children having accidents, but you can soften the fall when they land on a rubber surface. That means you're more likely to end up with a bruise than a broken limb. The secret is to make it soft enough to absorb some of the impact, but not so soft that the child still makes contact with what's underneath the rubber. What's more, we were offering wonderful bright colours to top them off and make children want to play there.

Fronted by Esther Rantzen, 'That's Life' was extremely popular receiving up to 15,000 letters from members of the public every week on consumer issues. For the record, they really were paper letters written with ink. This was the nineties. Esther was particularly affected by a letter from a mother whose daughter had fallen off the bottom of a slide in a public playground and fractured her skull. The programme researchers discovered that there was no system for officially collecting and collating statistics on playground accidents in the UK but that some countries were already using woodchip or rubberised surfaces to prevent serious injury.

She had one gimmick which really brought home the importance of safer playgrounds. Week after week on the show, she would drop one plate – or maybe it was an egg – on a square of rubberised material and another on a square of concrete. You probably won't need a PhD in forces and materials to work out what happened next. It created a huge consumer movement demanding better safety and Charles Lawrence Surfaces, armed with Playtop, was in the perfect position to take advantage of the demand. Then the insurance companies piled in, telling local authorities they would refuse to insure playgrounds which did not meet certain safety standards.

So what we did was to spend a small fortune getting outside experts to inspect and analyse our product to ensure that it met all the necessary local and national standards. It meant that if you were one of our licensees, you didn't just get high quality raw materials, but also all the certification to prove that it met the legal requirements. And you got one more ingredient in the mix – you got me. Please don't think that is some kind of conceited boast, it meant exactly what it said. If anything went wrong then you could be absolutely sure you had my personal guarantee that I would put it right. Not only did I mean that with absolute sincerity but, as I've said, that promise was to cost me a quarter of a million quid on a single big job.

Understandably, it was around this time that we just had too much work for me to do much of it myself. Although I loved the overseas travel, I took on a chap called Barry Baker as our Sales Director. Now he had been very senior at a rival company called En-Tout-Cas who had been in business since 1909 and were very much the early leader in artificial tennis courts. As you scholars will know, the name translates into English as 'in all conditions' which gave rise to the misnomer of the all-weather court.

Now unless you're a fan of tennis in a blizzard or a force 9 gale, then you can quite see there is no such thing as an all-weather court unless it happens to be indoors. In fairness, the trade descriptions act put an end to sloppy phraseology and En-Tout-Cas – whose name has survived but little else – like the rest of us adopted the expression 'all year round' surfaces. Well it was partly thanks to his work with his former employers that Barry Baker already had great contacts around Europe, Australia and New Zealand. He was an incredibly hard worker and rapidly began to build a network of licensees for all kinds of sports surfaces and playgrounds that we were offering.

We were growing very quickly, and new markets were opening up. Scandinavia got so busy on the playground side, we had to open an office there. I think it was in Copenhagen. But there were other developments overseas and a lovely family who had business in Porto, northern Portugal, became big customers of ours. They were already importing Volvo cars, vans and machinery but they took our business as well, bought some of our machinery and ran a highly successful outlet.

In fact the business was so successful overseas that in April 2006 Playtop won a Queen's Award for Enterprise in recognition of our contribution to Britain's international trade. The awards were first introduced in 1966 under the government of Prime Minister Harold Wilson and they are the most prestigious accolades in the British world of business – the business Oscars, if you will. Funnily enough, they were also yet another initiative of the sadly missed Duke of Edinburgh who chaired the founding committee. We received a very formal warrant signed by Her Majesty the Queen and Tony Blair, the Labour prime minister. For the next five years we were also allowed to fly a flag which showed we had been recognised for our outstanding work. I can tell you, we were all very proud indeed.

Alongside the playground stuff, we had also been doing sports pitches and running tracks from the late seventies. Nigel says we got our first running track commission for the Yarborough Sports Centre back in 1978. If you look on their website today, you will see they have a fabulous running track and swimming pool. The only thing that will have changed is that there will now be stringent health and safety controls around the kind of work which we were doing without any supervision, but we were innovating and, thank goodness, no one came to any harm.

Again, I'm relying on Nigel's memory when he says that our first full pitch contract was at Picton Sports Centre in Wavertree, Liverpool in 1981. Nigel says he remembers scrabbling the tender together over Christmas. I could go back over my records and check, but that would take too long so I'll take Nigel's word for it. At least the reason some of this is such a blur is, unlike Cirencester, where I was wearing my beer goggles, so much was going on that I was run off my feet and it was about to get even busier. But once more I am getting ahead of myself. I just hope I will have enough space in the book to fit it all in.

It is certainly worth recording that around this time, the Greater London Council (GLC) had its own technical department which set the conditions, decided on the specifications and ran the tests for all artificial surfaces being commissioned by councils all over the country. Now the only problem with them being judge and jury was that they got to choose the witnesses, write the evidence and pretty much decide on the verdict before the bloody trial had even started. So when they took a look at one of our tracks and said dismissively "That won't last a year", I couldn't help but put the record straight. It lasted 19 years before it needed refurbishing.

As I will come to explain later, I never wanted to be the cheapest, but I did always want to be the best. And without wishing to sound conceited, I think we were. But I was also sensible enough to realise that nothing would last forever. Thanks to an observation at an older running track, I was inspired to set up Replay Maintenance which used machines

Picking grapes at Stragglethorpe Hall – the most northerly white wine in England

With the Mayor of Lincoln – late seventies

to clean up all the sand and dirt on the artificial surface and make it serviceable for a few years more.

However, while the technology is fairly straight forward, the raw materials we had to work with could be temperamental, especially in the wrong weather. So let me tell you about the project that cost the company so much to fix. It was a big project in Wales working with the people who eventually bought me out – the Swiss-German company Conica. We had started laying the track, but the weather changed, and it was obvious we weren't going to get it finished so we contacted our supplier, Conica, and asked them what we had to do to maintain the integrity of what we had already done. They told us what to do and we complied.

The problem was, they had given us duff information and, when we returned in the spring, it was clear that the entire track would have to be re-laid. I contacted Conica who told me I would have to sort it out and I told them, rather plainly, where they could stick their raw materials. Anyway, I went to the council and told them what had happened but said I had given them my word that they could always trust me. Now this is what I have been talking about – the bill that my company paid was a quarter of a million pounds. Ultimately however, it paid a huge dividend because our reputation for honesty and decency became a by-word in the industry. Though the cost of doing the right thing still hurts.

Equally, a bit of sleight of hand has helped me out of trouble many a time. We laid one pitch and were all ready for the big handover with the local council officials when I suddenly noticed there was a large depression in the middle of the surface. I quickly told one of my guys to stand right in the centre of the dip and I would bring the officials over to meet him there, but I said that on absolutely no account, should he leave that spot. I duly marched the local bigwigs over the pitch and got them all standing in the hollow so they wouldn't notice it. The handover went perfectly and the second they had all gone, I got my guys to rectify the problem.

Although we had built our standing in the industry, it's only fair to say that artificial surfaces didn't always have a great reputation. Some of the earlier stuff like the ICI product, Olymprene, had been revolutionary in its time but there were also plenty of cowboys around who didn't do a particularly good job. What's more, when I saw some of the old plastic bristle type finishes, it was obvious that they quickly became just as hard and unforgiving as well as full of muck. It was clear we could develop machines which would clean up the old surface and leave it as good as new.

That's where the surface maintenance business came in. Using our engineering division, we ploughed money into designing machines which would clean the surfaces, returning them to looking fresh and perfect for play. We did have our setbacks, of course. We took one of our first prototypes to Nottingham University and tried to make it work – nothing. Then by accident, one of my chaps put it into reverse and hey presto – it worked perfectly. Don't worry, we managed to correct the fault.

But I was lucky to have the extraordinarily inventive and instinctive engineer Mark Keal working for me. Mark had joined straight from school at the age of 16 and had no formal engineering qualifications. But somehow, if I came to him with an idea for a new machine he could find a way to make it work and so, as I've said, Replay Maintenance was born. They are still in business cleaning and restoring artificial surfaces all around the world using compressed air to create a vortex and suck out all the dirt. After all, why replace a pitch for £150,000 when you can make it as good as new for a fraction of that price.

I have already said several times I never allowed budgets to stand in the way of progress when it came to creating new machines and it was genuinely exciting to pioneer new technology. Admittedly, we had a good few failures along the way, but the iron rule of business is that as long as you have more successes than disasters you stay afloat. Maybe I will call it my corporate Micawber principle though, unlike Dickens and me, Micawber was notoriously bad with money.

The sharp-eyed among you will have seen that I have titled this chapter 'Be Adaptable' and that is what we had to do next. There was one day when I was driving from Edinburgh to Newark, and I counted all the lorry tyres abandoned by the side of the roads. I reckon there must have been a couple of lorry-loads of tyres and while I can't claim I made an instant connection; it was pretty clear that here was an awful lot of abandoned rubber. You don't need a team of management consultants from Bain and Co to tell you that since the raw material for synthetic surfaces was also rubber, there was a piece of elegant corporate synergy at work here.

Recycling lorry tyres was the bright and bold new future.

Chapter Seven

*

Never give up

The smoke from the fire could be seen from miles away. A mate of mine called me from Lincoln and said he could see the black pall of burning rubber rising from where he was. To put it bluntly, a million quid's worth of investment in a lorry tyre recycling plant was going up in flames and it could have been the end of the story. However, since there are still a couple of chapters to go, you're all clever enough to realise that it wasn't. But I have to take you back a bit to explain how we got here.

Maybe, as has already been said, it was that eureka moment when I first touched the artificial surface fabric at ICI that pointed the way to the rest of my career in business. That's certainly Geoffrey's recollection of events and it's only fair to point out that if the two of us really do have something in common, it's the fact that we are both always right. Especially if we disagree. I'm glad that's sorted, let's move on.

When I looked at how much we were paying Horst Willnow for his rubber granules, I decided it was time to do something ourselves and that's when my gaze alighted on lorry tyres. Now without wishing to bore you, I can explain there is a big difference between car tyres and lorry tyres, and it comes down to this – lorry tyres have 30 to 40 per cent high grade steel in them. At first glance you might say, "So what?" but let me just explain that when you are mincing lorry tyres up to make rubber granules, you have a volatile mix of steel, which causes sparks, and rubber dust which is highly combustible. To all intents and purposes, you've just made a bomb.

Like most things in the world of business, my main motivation for getting into the tyre recycling business was financial. At the time we started looking at our own recycling venture, we were paying about £300 a tonne for rubber granules, and I thought that was bloody expensive. It would be pointless to pretend that I was some great eco-warrior out to save the planet and make Greta Thunberg happy; going into this new business area was a hard-headed, coolly calculated investment.

In fairness, that's a load of tosh too because I have always followed my instincts and, with the recycling, I just wanted to get into something new. Frankly, none of us had a clue how we were going to do it when we started, or how difficult and costly it would be. Though if you have come to understand anything about me so far, you will know that even if I had realised at the outset just how challenging it was going to be, nothing would have dissuaded me from trying anyway. As it turned out, it was – eventually – worth all the sweat and money we put in.

Speaking of money, there is one other aspect of this which is worth highlighting and that's the role of the international investment company 3i. They are a huge company with billions of assets under management and they had a particular interest in business and technology. That's why we brought them on board as a partner in the initial investment when we started the recycling. Again, this is one for you budding entrepreneurs – you have to make sure you have a secure funding stream when you're starting something new. 3i was a good fit for us at the time, though it's also important to say that we also bought them out again as soon as we could afford to because that gave us greater flexibility.

Our first challenge was to find the machinery to do the job. That took us to northern France and the sugar beet growing areas where one company made machines for shredding copper cable. Now the point here is that copper cable is quite soft, so I asked them if the machines could be used to shred tyres instead. Maybe this was just a question of misunderstandings arising from speaking two different languages, but they got together some rubber to prove it would work effectively. What we didn't specify was that we were going to be shredding lorry tyres with their high steel content.

Anyway, they seemed a nice enough bunch and I said, "How much for one of those?" and was told they were a quarter of a million quid each. So off I went to the bank where I had built up a surplus of about a million pounds and said, "Oy, I want to borrow a million so we can get into recycling." Bless them I got the money, which was just as well as I had already put in a firm order for the machines. It pays to have a bit of faith in yourself when it comes to business.

However, it wasn't quite as straightforward as that – we had to get the right premises for recycling which, because it's a noisy and dirty job, had to have special planning permission. Luckily, my nephew Nigel spotted a chance for us to buy up a scrap metal site on the Newark Business Park. Now handling scrap metal has the same restrictions as recycling tyres, so we were able to buy it and start the process of building the full plant, well away from any residential areas and hidden by a bank of soil. It was perfect.

Like I said, once I had embarked on a new project, I just wanted to crack on and start the recycling business. The great advantage of this business model was that you got paid twice; once for collecting the lorry tyres in order to get rid of them and the second time for the rubber granules which we could use for making artificial surfaces ourselves or selling them to our network of agents around the world.

We had been up and running for about a couple of months when Vanessa and I were driving to the south coast for a family party. The phone rang and it was Nigel telling me that the recycling plant was in flames and a giant pall of black smoke was drifting over the business park. Obviously, my initial reaction was to turn round and go back but Nigel persuaded me there was absolutely no point in that as there was nothing anyone other than the fire brigade could do.

It turned into one of the biggest fires seen in Newark since the Second World War and, at one point, there were up to ten fire engines battling to put out the blaze. It made headlines in the local media and by the end, all we had was a great charred mess of burnt-out machinery. The insurance claim was always going to be huge because we also had a massive bill for the cost of cleaning all the water channels which had been affected by the smoke and the burning rubber granules. To put it mildly, it was a right mess.

So, I hear you ask, as I stood side by side with Nigel looking over the ruins of our million-pound investment, did I ever think 'Sod this for a game of rubber soldiers, let's try something a bit easier?' Well, I can honestly say that not for one second, did I ever think of quitting at that point. We had deliberately set up the recycling business as a separate entity so that in the event of problems, it would not bring down the other businesses which were highly successful. But there was also my pride and stubbornness to factor in. There was no way I was going to be beaten, even after we had a second but smaller fire. So I thought, well if those machines can't do the job, we'll bloody well build our own.

The British economy was going through one of its periodic troubled phases in the early nineties with a recession under Prime Minister John Major's leadership which caused loads of properties to be repossessed when they couldn't keep up their mortgage payments. The trigger came in November 1992 with so-called Black Wednesday, when the government tried to prevent sterling crashing out of the ill-advised exchange rate mechanism designed to keep an artificially high parity between sterling and the German Deutschmark. It was doomed to failure and even pushing interest rates up to 15 per cent left the Chancellor Norman Lamont with more than a little egg on his face.

For us, it had a bit of a silver lining because we were able to buy a struggling engineering business in Newark, along with all the tools and machinery we needed for what became Charles Lawrence Engineering. Even I am prepared to admit it was a bold gamble since, at the outset, we had only a sketchy idea about how to overcome the issues we had faced with the first plant. What followed was many months of hard, often dirty and very hands on trial and error to develop what turned out to be a series of machines which would transform huge worn lorry tyres – known as super singles – into rubber granules.

The pioneering solution we came up with, was to have a series of machines which would progressively shred the rubber into ever smaller pieces, while at each stage removing some of the steel which could spark an explosion. The first shredder turned very slowly and would cut the tyres into pieces about six inches big and extract about 20 per cent of the steel. Then it went on down the line, each time the pieces got smaller until at the very end you had about 5 per cent of the steel still in the mix.

Now I'm not offering any prizes to the reader who points out that playground surfaces and football pitches with steel in them aren't going to be very comfortable if you come into contact with them. To solve this, the end of the line had powerful magnets which would pick up what was left of the steel and leave the rubber clean and safe. While I couldn't give you a guarantee that 100 per cent of the steel had been removed, it was rather like those adverts for bleach which promise to kill 99.9 per cent of germs but where they need to leave themselves some wiggle room. Well, I'm the same.

To be honest, it took us years to get the whole system right, but it sparked (no pun intended), a huge amount of interest around the world. It was an area where I can genuinely say that we were pioneers and it's here I need to pay full tribute to the engineering wizard who made a lot of it possible. I have already mentioned Mark Keal who joined

Vehicles outside the Charles Lawrence Group HQ Newark

Shaking hands with the King of Jordan, Sandhurst Military College 1980s

us as a young man with hardly any formal qualifications but who turned out to have a knack for making machines work which was truly extraordinary.

The outcome was that we could stop importing rubber granules through Horst Willnow and make our own for a third of the price. He wasn't too happy about that, but you've got to put your own business interests first. Mind you, even before we got the line working perfectly, we still had to produce rubber granules for our licensees. So we'd be in the plant at six in the evening with outstanding orders for ten tonnes of granules and a machine only spewing out two tonnes, just praying we could keep them all happy. It was a hell of a learning curve and I guess a lot of people would have just packed it all in, but we got there eventually. Thank goodness.

So now the orders were rolling in for raw materials, for the artificial surfaces we were laying in playgrounds and sports fields and now also for the machinery which we had created. Though we were happy to sell some of the machines, we would never sell an entire production line so we could keep hold of our commercial advantage and intellectual property. What's more, Geoffrey was able to use his legal knowledge to make sure we took out patents to cover all the innovations we were making and stay ahead of the game. So that's another note to budding business people – make sure you patent your ideas or someone else will nick them.

Also, make sure you are always open to new opportunities. There was one classic example of that when we were approached by Bass Breweries in Derbyshire who said they had a big problem in their massive warehouse. What was happening was that the forklift drivers were bumping into the steel pillars which were holding the whole thing up and that ended up with a lot of broken beer bottles. No problem, I told them, all we have got to do is coat all of the steel uprights with a generous layer of rubber granules and you can cushion any impact. We got the contract and they were delighted with the result. Job done.

This might just be as good a moment as any to give you an insight into what some would describe as my somewhat eccentric business practices – nothing X-rated but what I alone would consider perfectly normal. For this I am indebted to my excellent former personal assistant Joanne Hilbourne who worked with me for nearly three decades and has seen me at my best and, I have to be honest, at my sometimes, inebriated worst. Nonetheless, it must be testament either to her patience or my magnetic personality that she still works for the company – where she is now in senior management – and that she regards me as a good friend.

What she does say, is that I always had a great eye for the detail. Allow me to point out to anyone reading this who has an inclination to start their own business – it's great to have the big idea but if you don't pay attention to the small print, you will soon find yourself on the scrap heap. Jo claims that I would even point out the dust on the skirting boards, if the cleaners had missed it. While that might not be crucial to the bottom line, it showed that if I set high standards for myself, I expected the same high standards from those around me. I had a big window in my office from which I could keep an eye on almost everything that was going on at the plant and woe betide any slackers.

There is one other aspect of how I did business which Jo now laughs about when she comes to see me, and you may think it a trifle Luddite – I never owned a computer. I used to handwrite messages on paper and Jo would have to translate them. But it was a measure of my attention to detail that everything was colour coded – orange paper for emails and purple for faxes. My point is that it worked, and I can promise you, it didn't generate the wall of computer-generated emails where everyone and their dog is copied in. If you got a communication from me, you would know it wasn't spam. That in turn brought us some very good business.

One of the most prestigious contracts we ever won was to provide the foundations for the 2012 Olympic running track, as well as the machine which kept it clean. Perhaps I should make one small clarification in that we did all the groundwork and laid the basis for the track. But an Italian company called Mondo has an agreement which means they provide the surface for all Olympic tracks because they do it for free. However, I will always see it as our running track, and I was immensely proud of the part we played in what proved a hugely successful Olympic Games.

There is no single reason why we managed to get such good contracts but one contributory factor – and I am indebted to Jo for saying this – was that I had developed my own management style. Above all else, I found the most effective way of running a business was through observation and active listening. There were times when I would pop into the plant at two o'clock in the morning and have a chat with anyone who was there. Now on the positive side, that allowed me to get the lowdown on who the employees thought was a good, effective manager and how we could make the business more efficient. On the downside, I found one bloke sitting in the canteen who was supposed to be working. I sacked him then and there. I doubt if you'd get away with that these days, but you can't accuse me of being indecisive.

One other thing I truly believe is that knowing yourself and being free of any self-delusion are terrific assets in business. On the basis that too many people are promoted to their level of incompetence, I have had people working for me who were excellent at the job they were doing but seemed determined to seek promotion to a position they couldn't fill. One chap in particular, who I won't name, was an excellent surveyor who was convinced he should be more senior. Well, I warned him he was the wrong person but gave him a chance to prove me wrong. My instincts were correct and, unfortunately, he had to go too.

Speaking of listening to the views of other people, this is also a good time to flag up another idea which I would heartily endorse in the world of business – away days. Now I have to preface this by saying I loathe all the management speak about blue skies thinking and bloody 'granularity', but I am a great fan of plain talking and sharing ideas with other people who can bring their experience to bear on the issues. I've already said I'm a big supporter of good non-executive directors and that's why we would bring them all together at least once a year.

You have to step away from the workplace regularly because if you are living and breathing something every hour of every day, it's nigh on impossible to judge whether or not you are doing the right things at the right time in the right way. You already know I'm not really a hair-shirt kind of guy so we would book somewhere really nice where they could offer good food and wine and go over a wide range of issues. The non-execs would get to fire questions at us saying "How about this?" and "Have you thought of that?" and often enough, we would have to say, "Well no, we haven't". On occasions, they even persuaded me not to do something I had my heart set on. But it was first class teamwork. One other thing, we always noted the discussion and went back over what we had said when we next met to make sure we had done the things we said we would do.

We also used to have monthly division and board meetings to make sure we had a real grasp of what every part of the business was doing. Sometimes, people would get really fed up with it all and say they'd already gone through this before. To which I would say well you're bloody well going to go through it again. Equally, though I'm no Hitler, if someone was rambling on a bit in a meeting I'd just tell them to get on with it or what I found equally effective, was to tell them to shut up. It wasn't nasty and usually ended in a laugh, but it is so important to keep control of any meeting.

Mind you, there are times when the details really don't interest me. There was once a board meeting when I got so bored, I fell asleep, and someone had to tap me on the arm to wake me up. In fact, I usually managed to pay attention and Richard Hills, who was our Financial Director, has been kind enough to say that I always had a really good understanding of the numbers even though I am entirely self-taught. Or rather, Richard helped me to understand the theory and I got stuck into the practical bits.

One of the areas which I always checked was bad debts. I would heartily advise anyone who wants to make their business a success to keep a very close eye on debtors and make sure you chase anyone who hasn't paid up. Funnily enough, I was recently talking to a chap who was doing some work at my house and asked him if he'd been paid by the main contractor and when he said he hadn't, I asked him if he'd submitted his invoice. He looked a bit sheepish, so I assume he hadn't, and I gave him one of the 'Charles Lawrence Maxims for Good Business Practice' – the job's not over until you've been paid.

Though I suppose there are always the occasional exceptions, like when I did a tennis court for Sir Terry Wogan and he hadn't settled the final bill. So I called him up and told him to listen up. I said I would waive the rest of the bill if he came over to Newark and did the official opening of the recycling plant. Now knowing how much some of these buggers charge for that kind of thing, I'm pretty sure it was a bargain, and he was great fun to have around. Though I was a bit put out when he asked why the bloody hell I lived in a place like Newark. We love Newark.

We also had a funny run in when Sir Cliff Richard wanted a synthetic grass surface for his house in Barbados. I priced it up and said we would ship all the materials out in a container. Well, blow me down his agent came straight back and said the price was fine but since the container wouldn't be full, they'd like to fill the rest of it with a shipment of wine. Well, I happened to know that the port authorities in Barbados could be dreadfully slow and I wasn't prepared to vouch for the quality of the booze once it had finally been released from the port, so I said no. As it turned out, I was right and my man Jock, who went to do the job, had to wait ages for the materials though he wasn't complaining as he ended up living in Sir Cliff's rather lovely house until he could actually do the work.

This is also a good moment to share one other insight with you because it was one of the best business openings which we never took, but which would have made us a lot of money. Basically, the bank manager said he was prepared to advance me £300,000 to buy a big plot of land on the Newark Industrial Park, right next to where we had our existing premises. But when I took it to the board, they were all against it and though I fought hard to persuade them, they wouldn't budge and insisted it was too ambitious at that time.

To be honest, I was pretty hacked off because all my business instincts said it was the right move at the right time. But since I have argued how important it is to have a strong board, it would be contradictory to ignore their collective voice when they speak. Just let me say that Conica, who bought the business off me, now have to rent the same plot off the owners and the site itself is certainly worth millions. While I am not a man to hold a grudge, I certainly will never let them forget how wrong they were.

On a more positive note though, there was also one other development on recycling to mention here. At the outset, we would take all the steel we extracted from the tyres to landfill. We came to realise in later years that the stuff we were throwing away would fetch as much as £2000 a tonne – more than the rubber. So we worked with an Italian company – which has since gone bust – which had a system for grading the steel and turning it into ten-millimetre strips which the construction industry could use for making reinforced concrete. The waste product became the most lucrative part of the whole process.

Chapter Eight

*

Know when it's time to move on

When it comes to business, it's never easy to know when it is the right time to leave. There are no stage directions saying 'Exit stage left' or yawns from your host when you seem to have outstayed your welcome. You see, when you're running your own business, there is no finish line with cheering crowds and a gold medal presentation. There is only the way forward, the next business opportunity, the next technological innovation. The one thing on which I can give you an absolute guarantee is that I'm really glad I didn't jack it in any sooner. As in comedy, good timing is everything.

We did have several approaches to buy us out over the years which we did seriously consider at the time. In 2003, we got a call from the hygiene people PHS and Richard Hills assures me their MD paid us a call on Christmas Eve the same year – which shows that either they were very determined, or the boss was having a really miserable yuletide. Either way, we had a very productive meeting since they had, at that time, a small playground business as an offshoot of the hygiene products they make.

They are a huge company so I don't think I can have scared them too much with the kind of figures I was talking about if they wanted to buy us out. But it is in the nature of business that you have to roll with the punches and though we might have walked away with pockets full of cash at the time, as it turned out they lost interest. Well, they certainly went back to their toilets, while we set our sights on another decade of growth and development. I can't help thinking it was a lucky escape.

The next knock on the door turned out to be part of an extraordinary saga which ultimately sent shock waves throughout the artificial surfaces industry and could have been a disaster for the company we had so painstakingly built. First though, I will have to give you a bit more background. I've already said that one of the highlights of the industry's calendar was the biennial trade show in Cologne where everybody who was anybody – and quite a few who were nobody – came together to get utterly sozzled on my booze. By which I mean, of course, that these stalwart and upright denizens of our business united in perfect harmony to make deals and socialise. You can take your pick.

Well in the late eighties and early nineties, about the biggest bull in the field of artificial surfaces was the German company Balsam AG which was led by a somewhat larger-than-life character by the name of Friedl Balsam. I only met him a couple of times at the Cologne shindig, but we knew and respected each other in the business world and I certainly knew a lot of his underlings, who for the most part, were very friendly. They certainly seemed happy to come to my stand for the evening liquid negotiations.

By comparison with this German giant, we were still relatively small players, but we had developed machines for recycling tyres and for cleaning artificial surfaces which were definitely better than anything which Balsam could offer. So, they came sniffing around us with a view to a buy-out. Again, I suppose we could eventually have walked away with a bag full of cash but what we were about to find out is that we had the most spectacularly lucky escape from their clutches. If we had been tempted by their Deutschmarks, I can almost guarantee you that today there would be nothing left of my business.

On the face of it, Balsam was a hugely successful enterprise which employed 1,500 people worldwide and had a turnover of nearly £200m a year. In other words, I may have been the godfather of the industry, but Herr Balsam was definitely Big Daddy. Then in June 1994 came the news that rocked the whole business. Balsam's four-man management team was arrested on charges of fraud, tax evasion and forgery aimed at covering up years of losses from normal operations by gambling – would you believe it – on financial derivatives. Now on the issue of derivatives I am very much with Warren Buffett, the billionaire investor and 'Sage of Omaha' who said he never invested in anything he didn't understand. Balsam would have done well to heed his words.

It turned out that Balsam had been bankrupt since the mid-nineties, but its chief financial officer admitted that he had been submitting forged invoices for work which they had never done, through the factoring company

Procedo. Now factoring companies assume responsibility for collecting debt owed to their clients and in this case, they had paid hundreds of millions of pounds to Balsam for orders that didn't exist. I love the fact that once the news broke a spokesperson for Procedo said, "We found out a couple of days ago that something was amiss." Now you understand why I studiously checked every invoice, cheque and contract.

In the end, the scandal cost the German banks and insurance companies more than £1bn and marked the end of Balsam. Sadly, that did mean the loss of lots of jobs but on the positive side, it meant a lot more work for those of us who were still in business and to be fair, I took on some of their ex-employees. It also opened the way for yet another approach by a potential buyer – this time Balsam's main German competitor Polytan. Now given what had happened with their rival, it won't surprise you to know that we gave them very short shrift.

The collapse of the company did have a slightly amusing postscript though. When they came to flog off everything that was left of the company, I flew out to Germany for the sale to see if there was anything useful for my business. I popped into their very swanky offices and couldn't resist a quick trip to Balsam's personal bathroom. But when I had flushed the loo and come back out his personal secretary – who knew me – went absolutely ballistic that I had dared to trespass on her old boss's personal space. I thought it was a fitting tribute.

Anyway, business called me home and, as always, I was still keeping my eye out for the next opportunity and, as it happens, it came from north of the border. Anyone who has been to Scotland will have noticed one or more of the thousand trucks owned and run by the Malcolm Group. It is a family business with interests in transportation, construction, rail, maintenance and now – surfaces. It was a couple of years after Balsam had gone down the pan and they were keen to expand their interests in the South and they wanted to use my name as one of the main selling points – which I have to say was both flattering and lucrative. At that stage, Charles Lawrence Surfaces was the largest part of the group with turnover topping £12m a year and it was comfortably profitable.

They were just as bluntly spoken as I was – though maybe they threw in a few more expletives than I might have used. But it was the right time and the right price, so it was not a hard decision to make. Up until then, we had actually been competing because I had set up another company called Charles Lawrence Scotland, although that wasn't profitable, and I had to close it down. However, we did the deal with Malcolm Group and the original business of what subsequently became the Charles Lawrence Group, now had new owners.

What I had forgotten, until Richard Hills reminded me, is that along with keeping the name Charles Lawrence Surfaces, I also had to stay on as a director because they thought I could offer them some continuity and contacts. So I hung on in there for another five years, though I was sad to see that during those years, many of the extremely able team they had inherited from me left the company. As I have said before there is no place in business for sentimentality but I certainly think there should always be plenty of space for good people.

At least that left us free to focus on the businesses which

were still part of the group and that still included recycling, the machines we built ourselves, the maintenance work called Replay and finally the playground surfacing using the trademark Playtop. As I've said, thanks in particular to Esther Rantzen's campaign for safer playgrounds, Playtop was hugely successful and another profitable business. Two guys who were already licensees of ours made an approach and said they wanted to buy us out. Now, I was well disposed towards both of them because they always took us for a pre-Christmas lunch at the Ivy, in West Street, London. You may have heard of it because it's a great place for celebrity spotting but before you book, I should warn you that Dover Sole is on the menu for £43 a pop or if you've feeling skint, you can have Shepherd's Pie for a mere £19.50.

Anyway, I told these guys that while I wouldn't sell them the company, they could become licensees throughout the UK, but they would have to buy the rubber from me – which seemed to suit them fine, and we did a deal. But here's a word of warning to anyone going into negotiations with me, or anyone else, for that matter. Never turn up for the talks in a brand-new Bentley. After we signed the deal, I said to this chap that turning up in such a flash car added another half a million to the sale price, which left him looking rather flustered and at a loss for words. It's just basic psychology.

Again, that allowed us to focus on the rest of the business and make sure it kept on growing. However, like I said at the start, so much of life is about timing and I now had a Greek chorus of voices telling me it was time for me to take a bow and leave the stage. The chorus was led by my wonderful wife, Vanessa, with vocal support from my stepdaughter Sally but when even my bank manager chimed in that I couldn't go on for ever, I may be stubborn, but I knew I had to listen. But handing over the reins when you've been driving the cart for half a century is no easy task.

Once the board had agreed that it was the right time to sell the recycling business, we contacted a specialist firm who put you in touch with potential buyers. They drew up a long legal agreement and started the search. However, it was Nigel who again came up trumps by identifying Conica, the Swiss-German company with whom I had fallen out over the problems with the Welsh running track, as a potential suitor. He gave the name to the corporate specialists and they did the rest.

In many ways, Conica was the ideal new owner because they already had a global presence in sports surfaces and had a huge factory in Schaffhauzen, Switzerland. They also have sales offices in China and the USA – both markets I had been unwilling or unable to penetrate. Because they are a family-owned company, it also seemed to me that we would share the same approach to people and indeed, they would have the integrity to maintain the reputation and regard which I genuinely believed we had built over twenty years. We had got the licences back for Playtop by then, so they took on the recycling, the Playtop playground surfacing and the manufacturing.

Even though they were in many ways an ideal match, as I admitted at the very start of this volume, it was a terrible wrench for me personally to sell the company and I did not find the transition to my new life easy. Though as you will find in the next chapter, the pain of losing the business did allow me to find out what really mattered in life. I know it

Carrying out the "Winterbottom Test" on a synthetic turf football pitch in
Scotland 1980s

might sound a bit trite but top of that list is my family as I
will go on to explain.

However, we were still left with Replay Maintenance
which was a completely separate undertaking based on
a nearby airfield and by far the most profitable of all the

different businesses. There I opted for a Management Buyout (MBO) and gave them three years to pay off the existing shareholders. Since the business already had a million quid in the bank, it was a bit of a fatted calf, but I'm delighted to say that it has continued to grow and prosper. In fact, I only severed all connection in April 2020 and the new owners remain friends which has got to be a good sign.

All of which rather brings me back to where I started. When I sold off recycling, I was 75 years old and although still in good health, Vanessa had persuaded me that it was time to enjoy more of the fruits of my labour. But it's important that I stress for anyone keen to pursue a similar trajectory that as far as my business life is concerned I do not harbour a single regret. I always loved being the first one in the office, greeting everyone who worked there by name, checking the accounts and keeping tabs on any debtors. I loved working with Mark Keal to make new machines and never minded getting dirty hands to get it all working, if that was necessary. It was all part of the fun.

In fact, there is a story I'd like to share with you that will give you an insight into the way I have always worked. The new owners asked me if I would come in and look at a new recycling machine they had just installed to make sure everything was up to my standards. So I had a really good look at this machine and nearly everything was fine. However, at the end of my inspection I turned to their chief engineer and said, "Sorry mate, you haven't welded on the inside of that joint over there." I won't tell you what he said in reply, but we had a good laugh about it.

But though my work life had been a great roller coaster of a ride, it's fair to say that nothing comes without a price.

Especially during my younger years, I would always work seven days a week, never taking a holiday and constantly chasing the next contract while at the same time worrying about the money. With hindsight, I don't quite understand how a young man in his early twenties with very little business experience could have run an operation with up to 30 men mowing, cultivating, planting, landscaping and often misbehaving. But as the title of the book says – I did it.

Now as I look back, I can see that in part I paid for it with the turmoil of my private life. I have never been in the regrets business and have no wish to lacerate myself with loads of what might have been, but I know it must have been hard for my family. Building a business would take its toll on anyone, but at least I was always in the thick of the fight and enjoyed it. As in any battle it's the non-combatants you have to feel really sorry for. In my case they were my three wives and my three children – I say three because my stepdaughter Sally is as close to me as any child of my own.

Come on now Charles, you're getting all maudlin and I can't have my grandchildren knowing what an emotional old bear I can be. But I can tell you honestly, the next chapter will be the most difficult to write because it demands a degree of vulnerability and openness which I could not have shown as a young man and which is still hard even in my eighties. But as the old Mastermind grand inquisitor Magnus Magnusson used to say: "I've started...so I will finish." Here goes.

Chapter Nine

*

Understand what is important

It must have been more than half a century since I last walked through the front gate and into the cemetery of St Mary the Virgin's parish church in Bottesford, which is only 20 minutes drive from my home. The impressive spire seems to pierce the sky above the overgrown and rather neglected churchyard. But it's a place that inspires reflection rather than melancholy and the jumble of gravestones says so much about the history of this area, not least the collection of memorials to RAF Lancaster Bomber Crews who had flown from this area to their deaths.

The last time I was there, I was with my mother and it's a funny trick of the memory, I can still recall that occasion. This time, it was with my wife Vanessa and I was on the trail of a piece of my family history. Despite the passing years and the fact that the graveyard is quite a large sprawl of a place, I recalled exactly how to get to the grave I was looking for. Indeed, there it was, exactly where I had expected it to be. There were a few weeds growing through the greenish marble chips, but the headstone was that of my maternal grandmother Charlotte Jane Taylor who died in 1958 aged 78 and grandfather Frederick who had passed away, aged 82, in 1953. I can't deny I felt quite emotional, but another piece of the puzzle was in place.

Like I said, it's really hard to write about personal stuff but I feel it is right to pay tribute to all those members of my family who have stuck with me through the bad, as well as the good. Being a successful entrepreneur does not come without a cost and long hours, frequent absences and grumpy moods are all part of the landscape. Fortunately, I have now lived long enough to have a better sense of perspective on what really matters, and I really do want to say a huge thank you to my family and friends.

Right at the outset of this book, I traced the family back on my father's side, but I had been somewhat less successful with my mother's relatives. My mother Peggy Eileen Taylor, who was universally known in the family as Tootie, was born in the town of Chesterton in Cambridgeshire in 1911. While I have no clear idea how my parents first met, I have said that my grandfather Frederick worked at the Clinton Arms. Therefore, it's reasonable to suppose that's where my father first saw my mother. But we will never know for sure. Maybe the really surprising thing is that since eligible men were in such short after the First World War, it's amazing he didn't marry sooner. So, what can we deduce about my mother's family?

Thanks to online records, I have been able to trace my mother's family back to the 1881 census, when the family was living at 11 Bridge Place in Southampton. It seems my maternal great grandmother Caroline was then 22 and married to the 26-year-old Thomas Wilson, who gives his occupation as a Foreman Moulder at the ironworks. Caroline describes herself as a tailoress who was born in Bath, Somerset. By then they already had two children: John and my maternal grandmother Charlotte Jane. Sadly, Caroline died before the century was out having given birth to three more children.

By the 1901 census, the family was living at 27 Union Road, Southampton with my maternal great-grandfather now describing himself as an Iron Founder. His children John (23), Charlotte (21) and Florence (19) are all described as single and living at home. The younger siblings William (16) who is working as a joiner and George (14) who is an office boy mean the house must have been bursting at the seams. Especially once you include Sarah, his 74-year-old Irish mother who had come to live with them from Dublin, presumably to lend a hand with childcare.

We next catch sight of my mother's family in 1911 – the year my mother was born. My grandparents Charlotte Jane and Frederick William Taylor had married in 1905. For some reason, Charlotte is shown living with a licensed victualler (in other words a publican) called Mary Gerard in Chesterton, Cambridgeshire. The widowed 46-year-old Mary was clearly managing the pub well, since she had two live in servants, 30-year-old Marguerita Green and 16-year-old Lily Barnard. Perhaps they were looking after Charlotte until my mother was born in Chesterton.

One other small detail I would like to add is that my grandmother's younger sister, Florence, was to marry a man called Page. Now they had a son called James who in turn, called his son James Page. Now that James Page restyled himself as Jimmy Page and became guitarist and founder of the legendary rock band Led Zeppelin which means I am distantly related to rock royalty. On the other hand, my mother's father Frederick has disappeared from the records and I can find nothing more about him.

What I do know, however, is that when I was a teenager, my sister Valerie – who was born in 1932 – was already dating a haulage contractor called Leonard. They used to take me to the speed track at Long Eaton when I came back for the school holidays and I absolutely loved that. They had speedway racing there on and off from 1929 to 1997. For those who don't know, speedway bikes have no brakes, only one gear and their 500cc engines allow them to accelerate faster than a Formula 1 car. You can see why I enjoyed it and can only hope that my sister did too.

In those early days, my sister worked at a department store in Nottingham called Griffin and Spalding which was eventually swallowed up by Debenhams. Back then, it was a wondrous emporium with a long history. Founded in 1846 by the brothers Edward and Robert Dickinson as what is quaintly called a drapery store. It was bought by Messrs Griffin and Spalding in 1878 and they expanded it by purchasing stores in Market Street and Long Row. By the time my sister worked there, it had been completely remodelled and comprised 37 trading floors covering all manner of goods. In an early example of good marketing (eat your heart out John Lewis) they offered ten bob (50p in your modern money) to the first person who could tell them a competitor was selling something cheaper.

Once my sister had got out of the department store, she started a family. She and Leonard had two children, Nigel, who I've told you came and worked with me, and his younger sister Louise who is a lovely, gentle soul. Sadly, my sister and her husband drifted apart, and she had to find work taking care of a wealthy farming family. We used to have Christmas celebrations at her house in Southwell, rather charmingly called Wilderness. However, I can't say we were a terribly close family and anyway, I was working almost every day of the calendar landscaping and cutting grass by then.

My niece Louise talks very affectionately about my mother who always worked hard to keep the family together – almost as hard as she did tending her garden at Manor Cottage. She always was something of a horticulturalist and took a diploma at Brackenhurst College at Nottingham Trent University. We certainly always got together for my mother's birthday on August 10th when she would break out the Pimm's by way of celebration.

As for my own family, well you've heard me say before that I am not given to regret as it doesn't serve any useful purpose. But as I reflect on more than eight decades of life, I would have liked to have had less turbulence in my personal affairs. In marital terms, it seems rather trite to say third time lucky, but I can honestly say that on that front, I have never been happier or felt more fulfilled, than I am now with Vanessa. But that doesn't mean that I didn't get a lot of positive energy from my first two marriages and I'm delighted to say that my first wife and I are still on good terms.

So that is where I am going to start. Maybe we were a bit too young to get hitched, but in 1969 when I was in my mid-twenties, as I mentioned at the start of this narrative,

I married the beautiful young Valerie Hyde. It's funny now when I think of it, I must have come across as a bit of a flash git with my booming business and my love of fancy cars. Well, if that's the impression I gave, so be it. The truth is that I have always been quite a simple soul with very few pretensions and a very down to earth view of people and life. Richard Hills was kind enough to say that I could talk just as easily to a duchess or a peasant but that when push came to social shove, I'd rather spend my time with the peasant. I think he's spot on.

We had a lovely wedding and a very jolly reception after which I bought a charming 18th century seven-bedroom house called Grey Garth on the high street of the equally charming village of Brant Broughton (pronounced Brewton) about eight miles from Newark. It cost me £4,500 and it had a large garden which was perfect once the girls were growing up.

It seemed like no time at all before we had two adorable little girls, Sally and Julie, and I am guessing that on the face of it, we looked like a model couple. The reality was rather more complex. I've admitted that in the early seventies, despite the fact that I was working dawn till dusk, the business was a real challenge. Now whether it was the problems at work which were making homelife difficult or the other way round, I honestly couldn't say. Whichever it was, our relationship paid the price and after six years together, we decided to go our separate ways.

Unless you have been through it yourself, it's impossible to fathom the emotional turmoil which comes with divorce, especially when there are children involved. Figures show that one in five marriages ended in divorce back in the seventies compared with one in three twenty years later. But every one of them has its own tale of heartache and ours was no exception, though I did have Sally and Julie every weekend and did my level best to be a good father to them.

When they were little, we loved going horse riding on a Sunday morning at Saxilby Riding School near Lincoln for a two-hour hack. It was a wonderful family time and I cherished it. Then it was off to the Albany Hotel carvery in Nottingham for a wonderful traditional Sunday lunch. My stepdaughter Sally teases me that I used to encourage them to nick the little soaps from the ladies' loos and insists they would get into the car with hotel cutlery stuffed up their sleeves. Well, I suppose we might have done it for a laugh.

These days, of course, both the girls are grown up with families of their own. My eldest daughter Sally started her career in hospitality and had a job at a local up-market country house hotel where, in fact, she met her future husband. She had worked previously in Australia and persuaded her husband to move there together with their one-year-old son Joe Max. They are now happily settled on the north east coast of Queensland and have taken Australian citizenship. A second child was born out there – lovely Amy Jade. We have had some wonderful trips "down under" to see them and enjoy adventures together including to Uluru and the Great Barrier Reef. It's just sad that we can't see them more often.

Happily for us, my second daughter Julie has stayed rather closer to home. She has always been wonderful with children and worked in a children's nursery and as a Teaching Assistant in a primary school for many years. Her partner, Trevor, has supported her for over twenty five years through the good and the bad. It's funny that I'm completely surrounded by females as she has two lovely daughters – Ella and Olivia. Ella is extremely bright and has a very tough job running a haven for youngsters with problems. She had to put her wedding plans to the admirable Jay on hold during the pandemic but they have given me my first great grandchild, the adorable Ada Violet. Me a great-grandad – who would have believed it?

Olivia works with adults with learning disabilities. Isn't it strange that both my daughters (Sally in Australia now works with Aborigine children in difficulties) and two of my granddaughters work in the caring profession? It is something of which I am very proud. Olivia has teamed up with a delightful young man, by the name of Lloyd, who is a qualified butcher with plans to set up his own business.

Any parent wants to protect their children from harm and I am incredibly proud that Julie has tried so hard to overcome the troubles that have beset her over the years. That's why one of the key illustrations in this chapter is Julie's montage of me in gardening mode. She says it encapsulates how she thinks of me so I am delighted I come across as a rather jolly individual – spade and all.

The other female in my life is my step-daughter, Sally, who came into my life when she was about three years old after I had met her mother Pat. Now Pat was a stunningly attractive woman but underneath it all, was a complete bundle of nerves. Our courtship wasn't entirely straightforward either. For instance, there was the day I was going back to Brant Broughton and I was a bit worried people would see Pat in the car, so I persuaded her to hide in the boot.

Well you might think that on its own was odd enough,

but it got a lot weirder. There had been some sheep rustling in the area and the police had set up a makeshift roadblock. So I'm pulled over by the police who not unreasonably asked if they could they have a look in the boot. Well, I can tell that explaining the presence of a beautiful blonde in the boot of my car taxed even my powers of persuasion, but I must have come up with something vaguely plausible because they sent me on my way.

Not long after that, we set ourselves up in a new house just opposite my mother in Hawton. I'd got a contract to knock down the old rectory in the village and once that was out of the way, the site was redeveloped, and I bought one of the houses which had been built there and called it Cranleigh House. It might seem a bit perverse of me since I have told you how much I hated my school days at Cranleigh but for what it's worth, my current house is called Cranleigh Park so I may be perverse but at least I'm consistent.

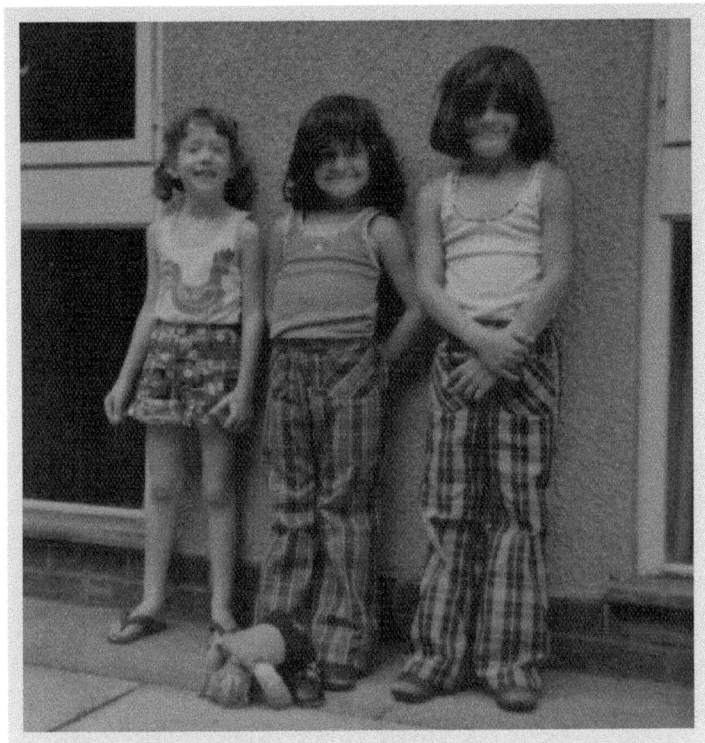

My step daughter Sally with my daughters Julie and Sally at
Cranleigh House, Hawton

It was a measure of just how hard I was working at that
stage, that I almost missed my wedding to Pat. I was out
fixing a puncture in a tractor tyre when I suddenly realised it
was nearly time to be at the registry office. As it was, I legged
it back and got there just in time for the "I do" bit and then
went straight back to work. I know it doesn't sound terribly
romantic, but we didn't even have a reception and I'm afraid
the old adage of marry in haste, repent at leisure was probably
thought up with us in mind

Montage of me as a gardener by my daughter Julie

When I first entered Sally's life, she said she knew me as the man who brought the tomatoes. Now that might strike you as a somewhat eccentric courting ritual, but it was clearly effective. To begin with, Sally always called me Uncle

Jim and says I introduced a system where I fined her every time she called me that. Instead, I got her to call me by one of my middle names – Seager – after the brand of gin which had such a soothing effect on the wartime crowd at the Clinton Arms. For her I am Seager to this day.

For all the stress, Sally does have some happy memories of childhood including trips to Scarborough to play on the beach. There was even an outing with a caravan which she describes as an unmitigated disaster and it certainly wasn't repeated. And it can't have been half as traumatic as the day Sally cut her foot and screamed and bled all the way back to the car. I've never let her forget that you can be sure.

Now, I will use Sally's words for what happened to us next because it remains one of the enduring mysteries of the human soul that you must never take outward appearances for anything more than that. The way Sally puts it, is that while on the face of it her mother had so little to worry about, she was in fact a bundle of anxiety and self-doubt. These days, in part thanks to the royal princes William and Harry, it's becoming so much easier to admit issues surrounding depression and mental health. Back in the seventies and eighties there was still a lot of stigma attached and so the Prozac generation was born.

It amazes and delights me when I see what a wonderful, thoughtful and well-balanced person Sally is today, that she has come through the trials of her mother's personal struggle and found her own still point of the turning world. That's despite the fact that once her mother and I had parted company, Pat turned for comfort to Buddhism and was very involved with the movement. I had bought her a house of her own while I stayed on in splendid isolation at Cranleigh

Park. But it's a measure of the generosity of Pat's spirit that having told me she knew she could never make me happy, she suggested I take up with the woman who has brought such comfort and fulfilment to my life – Vanessa.

You see Pat had bumped into Vanessa when she was in London and could tell that I had found her extremely attractive, so it was her idea that I asked her out. To say I was intimidated would be an understatement, but I eventually plucked up my courage, put on the full suit of Lawrence charm and invited her to dinner. Unfortunately, she rather cooled my ardour by saying 'Thanks but she had a cold' so could not oblige. Equally, it's simply not in my make-up to take no for an answer and I eventually got that dinner date. The rest as they say…

However, as Buckingham Palace said after the Sussexes' interview on Oprah Winfrey, 'recollections may vary'. It's always fascinating to compare what each of you remembers and Vanessa insists that, at the time of my initial offer of dinner at the Dorchester, she was actually very ill with a bronchial infection and needed a couple of weeks off work. I defer to her better recall on that and the suggestion that she doesn't really remember the first time we ever met – not even the thunderbolt which must have struck her. However, she does recall that I was a regular presence at meetings which she also attended as Membership Director of the Sports and Allied Industries Federation.

What's more she remembers me as a gentleman. Back in those days, it was standard practice for people – admittedly mostly men – to smoke whenever and wherever there was an opportunity. Personally, I had a weakness for small cigars or cheroots which I thoroughly enjoyed. However, Vanessa remembers one particular meeting at Worcestershire Cricket Club when I insisted that if anyone wanted to smoke, they had to go out on the balcony to protect her from the noxious fumes. Happily, they all did as they were told, and Vanessa was rewarded with a smoke-free environment and they got to gaze at Worcester's lovely cathedral rising proudly above the River Severn.

Anyone who knows my character, will also understand that I am nothing if not persistent and I continued to show my affections for her. She recalls one Christmas when we were at a meeting at the Royal Agricultural Society in Kenilworth, and I told her I had something for her in the car. Now she was fine about the bottle of champagne I gave her but was distinctly underwhelmed when I pulled a Christmas card out of its wrapping and started to fill it in as I hadn't had time to do the niceties earlier. Women are such sticklers for that kind of stuff.

Anyway, after a number of years working together, we finally got close, and I used to nip down to her place near Stratford-upon-Avon at the weekends to woo her. That lasted quite a while, but Vanessa was having a hard time at work and found herself out of a job. Although she went on to work on a project to found a new hospice in Stratford (called imaginatively the Shakespeare Hospice) she went through a period of ill health, which laid her low. At this point, she said, I charged into view as her white knight and suggested she came to live with me in Newark. Good call Charles.

Bizarrely, she says she thought I was a bit of a wide boy and never thought we'd get married in a million years. On the contrary, I had a shorter time frame in mind and so waited for a weekend when we had gone to one of our favourite places – Holkham Beach in Norfolk, one of the most unspoilt and beautiful stretches of sand in the country. I just felt it was the right time to pop the question but wasn't in a hurry – much to Vanessa's irritation. In fact, I was a bit nervous.

Anyway, I did get there eventually and that evening (in the kitchen at Cranleigh Park) got around to the question-popping. Now on the plus side, she did say yes without a huge amount of hesitation. On the down side, I suggested we could use a diamond ring I had given her the previous Christmas as our engagement ring. Now it seemed to me that I was sensibly and thriftily repurposing a rather handsome three diamond piece of jewellery as a genuine love token. Apparently, that's not considered wildly romantic. Anyway, we were by now very settled in our relationship and comfortable with each other, so we set a date for the wedding.

This time I was determined to do things properly and Vanessa and I got married in June 2005 at the grade II listed Georgian hotel Langar Hall, 12 miles from Nottingham. I didn't want a lot of people, just four close friends with Geoffrey as my best man. The only issue we had was that the registrar was a real stunner, and it became a standing joke that I was going to do a runner with her. The truth is that I wouldn't have dared and since everyone was singing Vanessa's praises, I knew just how lucky I was.

We had a fabulous lunch with excellent wines and after a night at the hotel, we were chauffeured down to London to stay at the dear old Dorchester Hotel. I hope you will remember me telling you that it was my father's second home, and it has played a significant role in my life too. There is just something so very welcoming about the place and given that Vanessa was so posh – the de Pembertons can trace their history back to the time of Richard I – we fitted in just nicely. Even a rough old bugger like myself.

The following day we were off to join the Orient Express on its way to Venice for a proper honeymoon. I thought after three marriages we were both entitled to a bit of luxury, so we did the whole thing in style. As we did with subsequent trips going first class to Australia or around India on the Palace on Wheels luxury train. Mind you, I'm not so sure about the Norway cruise because we headed back in a force 12 gale and because we had the suite right at the top of the ship, we were pitching and rolling like a rowing boat in an Atlantic swell.

With hindsight, it seems quite an adventure. I had to have an injection for sea sickness and Vanessa sat downstairs in the bar drinking gin and tonics with Esther Rantzen – the tv personality who had publicised safe playground surfaces – while giant waves broke over the bow. What slightly rankled is that with sea water coming into the cabin from the balcony, the captain kept insisting that everything was fine. I can't help thinking that Captain Edward John Smith would have been proud of him. In case you were wondering – he was the captain of the Titanic.

The great thing is that Vanessa is a great organiser and socialiser while I'm a bit of a social tortoise who likes the calm and comfort of his shell. It is thanks to Vanessa though that we have gone out a lot more and because she is so outgoing, we have also been able to organise fundraisers for Cancer Research. She does all the hard work and I just tag along – though I am always useful when it comes to the charity auctions. However, I will return to this in my last chapter.

Those of us who are fortunate to have found what I have called before the still point of the turning world, (okay, I know a few poetry lovers will recognise it as a line by the poet T.S. Eliot) will no doubt wonder sometimes why we have been so blessed when we think of our parents' generation experiencing the trauma of not one, but two, world wars. Vanessa has been kind enough to say that I rescued her at a very difficult time and indeed, when she first came to Cranleigh Park she was too weak to walk around the gardens. This was her refuge, and it has been mine. It's a place of solace and repose, as well as giving me hours of satisfaction cutting the grass on my tractor. It has also been the location of many happy gatherings, bringing together both family and friends.

It's certainly a great excuse to have a bit of fun. I must admit that I did get a bit 'relaxed' at the boat show one year and ended up buying a cruiser, which could politely have been described as a gin palace. When it was delivered, it all looked rather impressive, but it was meant to be a sea-going vessel and had to restrict itself to the local River Trent. Frankly, I hadn't a clue what I was doing with the damn thing, but we did go on a few outings and I managed not to drown anyone, though I think the whole thing created a happy mixture of alarm and amusement in the family – so I sold it. Trouble is that after it had vanished to its new owners on a trailer, I remembered there were still four bottles of gin on board which I had forgotten to salvage – well I did say it was a gin palace.

At least cars have been less of a disaster area, though they have certainly cost me a fair penny over the years. One of my favourites was the Rolls Royce Corniche which I bought from someone we met in Spain. Vanessa and I were down on the Costa Brava with our chums when we met a dealer in African art who had taken possession of the car in settlement of a debt. It was a beautiful machine which had been bought new in 1972 by a Los Angeles wood merchant and I had the original bill of sale for £8000 including delivery. For the record, the last Corniches made by Rolls Royce were selling for a quarter of a million pounds each.

So, I said to this chap that if he ever fancied selling the car, I would buy it off him. Well a month later, I got a phone call asking if I was serious and once we'd agreed a price, the car was duly shipped to the UK. It's such a lovely convertible that it cried out to host couples getting married and indeed, our friends in Spain asked if there was any chance we could come back south and ferry their daughter to her wedding. Thanks to the can-do de Pemberton-Lawrence spirit, we were soon heading back through France to provide nuptial transportation – it's a pity about what happened next.

Apart from the handbrake failing on a steep hill, there was an even graver crisis heading our way. On the back seat was Vanessa's rather splendid and indeed rather wide-brimmed wedding hat. It was as we were crossing the Pyrenees with the top down that a wicked wind took hold of this millinery marvel and whisked it onto the road behind the car. I promise I was not indifferent to Vanessa's calls of distress but access to the rear-view mirror had already told me that a forty-tonne truck had already rearranged it as a far more two-dimensional object. You can imagine her sartorial dismay as the only woman at the wedding without a swanky hat.

Maybe it was to punish me, but I now have my own chauffeur's hat which I have worn to four weddings – I don't do funerals – and was usually available for a small fee. To be honest, the fee was an invitation to the wedding festivities.

Though I really did love that car, it was also blocking up a large part of the garage and has now found a new home. But it remains a testament to the great days of British motoring and indeed British engineering.

Perhaps all I can really say in conclusion for now, is that having family around you is probably the greatest comfort you can possibly have. Maybe I didn't always get my priorities right and I can only ask forgiveness for any of the speech days, sports competitions and family outings that I might have missed due to work commitments. It's easy to be judgmental when you are looking back over the space of years or even decades, it's far harder to plot a course when you're steering life's boat through the waves.

I just hope you can all find it in your heart to be charitable. I know I'm not perfect, but I did what I thought was right at the time and I certainly did it with every fibre of my body. In the end, you will be my judge.

Chapter Ten

*

Leave something behind

There I was, standing in front of a couple of hundred people and they're all roaring with laughter. What was even more remarkable is that I was laughing even more than they were – and I wasn't even sure if any the stories I was telling were actually true. While I've read that in surveys most people's biggest fears are death and public speaking, I can honestly say I have never had a problem with the second one and talking to large groups of people has stood me in very good stead in my public roles. Which is why my final chapter is on legacy.

Since I have already written about my family, I don't need to include them here, but I hope it goes without saying that they will always be my greatest joy. But this is about what else we can do to make our short stay in this world a bit more productive and give back some of the great blessings and benefits which we have received. Part of that is simply creating a business which has given employment to up to 100 people at any one time and encouraging unlikely and exceptional talents like the self-taught engineer Mark Keal.

But I'd like to think that one of the biggest contributions I have made is to the reputation and acceptance of the whole artificial surfaces industry. Back in the early seventies, the industry didn't have a great name not only because we had more cowboys than the OK Corral, but a lot of the early synthetic surfaces were awful. Once they got dirt in them, they would end up as hard as concrete so not surprisingly playing sports on them could be painful. So, I made it my mission to try and clean things up a bit – both literally and metaphorically.

To that end, I helped to found the Sports and Play Construction Association (SAPCA) in 1997 with two purposes in mind. The first, as I say, was to improve the image of the industry and the second was to have a single, effective voice to talk to government and lobby on behalf of all the companies and individuals in the sector. There were the usual mutterings about how it was yet another Charles Lawrence takeover plan as part of my scheme for world domination, but enough sensible people saw the need for such a trade body and SAPCA became a fixed part of the landscape.

The first chief executive was an excellent guy who was head of the technical side at the Lawn Tennis Association – a certain Chris Trickey, whose name belies his open and generous nature. I became chairman from the outset and stuck it out there until 2010 when they gave me a great send-off and a very large lump of crystal with my name on it. What we have ended up with is a far more professional, clean and transparent industry with high standards and good governance. It still amuses me that I was known as the Godfather of the artificial surfaces industry – don't worry it has no mafia connotations – because I was thought of as the 'go to' person who would have the answers. That was certainly the case with SAPCA.

What we did, and still do, is to use Experian as an independent credit assessor, to vet the finances of all member companies to ensure that they are financially solvent and always carried a bit of surplus funds in case things went wrong. (I am trying not to mention the Welsh running track again…) Members were – and still are – monitored on a monthly basis and if anyone doesn't come up to scratch then we give them a chance to put things right and if they don't, we kick them out. Trust me, I had some very difficult conversations with people over the years, but we have really built our credibility.

Chris Trickey is probably being too generous when he credits me with playing what he calls a pivotal role in the establishment and effectiveness of the organisation – personally I think a great deal of it is down to his excellent leadership over 25 years. But if there is a compliment going, I won't bin it. So he says we have created a disciplined, energetic and rigorous organisation which has transformed the image of the industry and set incredibly high standards. And that's partly because of what Chris says of my character which he describes as indefatigable, unstoppable and litigious. Like I said, I've never been afraid of a fight. He's also kind enough to say that along with that belligerence, we also always had time for some fun.

Now, when I think about it, we must have done something

right because we persuaded local government bodies only to accept quotes from SAPCA members which meant we had gone from cowboy status to law enforcement. Certainly, if you look at the SAPCA website today, you will see all the signs of a highly professional and polished organisation which sets very high standards for its members, breeds confidence in its clients and has expanded to take in all aspects of the industry.

But it's also true that although we have come a long way, there is still a lot of road ahead. SAPCA is constantly reviewing its strategy to ensure it remains relevant and fit for purpose. What I would like to think is part of my legacy, and this is something Chris suggested, is that the organisation has become the gold standard for the whole industry and membership is widely seen as a badge of quality. It's true that some sports have adopted synthetic surfaces more enthusiastically than others – hockey is an excellent example of an early advocate – but as the technology continues to advance, it seems likely others will climb aboard.

What that means is that the industry, in general, has a very bright future. Okay, the surface on which you play the game will never be as 'sexy' or worthy of headlines as the athletes who play on it. But we share a lot of common goals and know we must deal with the consequences of issues like climate change. We also have to ensure sustainability (I know it's the buzz word of the day) through sensitive environmental policies and ever more recycling. But I am delighted to say that with Chris at the helm, SAPCA has led the charge. It means the UK will remain a global leader long after I am pushing up rubber granules.

One other thing I'd like to mention. It's not why I did it, but I have to own up that setting up SAPCA did bring some personal benefits too. Thanks to my work with SAPCA, the Worshipful Company of Paviors, which is a Livery company in the City of London, gave me their annual award for contributions to the surfacing industry and nominated me as a Freeman of the City. The Paviors has been around since before 1276 and has been a Livery company since 1479 with the remit of looking after London's pavements. Though clearly, that's no longer its preserve, the Company does try to uphold best practice throughout the surfaces construction industry.

Now as some of you may know, from early times, everyone who wanted to trade within the square mile of London had to be a Freeman of the City. These days it is purely honorific, but it does still include the right to drive sheep across London Bridge and there is still a wonderfully colourful annual event when a flock of sheep does the journey as of old – though they are no longer immediately taken to a market and slaughtered. It's a wonderfully quaint and I think, rather charming ceremony which I had the privilege to take part in.

It's also thanks to my SAPCA connection that I got a chance to visit a rubber plantation on a trade trip to Malaysia. It was fascinating to see the raw material being harvested which I had worked with for so many years and to learn that rubber trees were first planted by the British in 1877 with plants from the Amazon basin. Today, ninety per cent of all the output is from smallholders with farms of 40 acres or less and though it all looked a bit chaotic to me, in fact it is a highly productive and efficient industry.

However, I am also very happy to be associated with anything that will benefit my beloved Newark and the people of the area. It's all very well Sir Terry taking the mickey out of my hometown, but it really is a terrific place inhabited by a lot of wonderful people – and a few dodgy ones, of course. By the way I am not referring to myself there. One of the best amenities in the area is the former airfield at RAF Winthorpe which since 1964 has been owned by the Newark and Nottinghamshire Agricultural Society.

Way back, the 200-acre site was used for the Newark May Fair, a tradition which fades into the mists of history. The May Fair was a celebration of everything to do with agriculture – particularly sheep – but it has expanded hugely since those days. When there is not a pandemic blighting the land, it is host to everything from the Newark Vintage Tractor and Heritage Show to the Antiques Fair and the Garden Show. One year we even hosted the European Juggling Convention, which I think shows the showground's flexibility and dexterity.

Now, I've been associated with the show for quite a while and in 2008 they must have been desperate to find someone to head the committee, so they asked me to be President. I can only assume awkward buggers must be in short supply in the area as they have asked me to do it again. But like I say, I am happy to do my bit for Newark and the show is a great event. It may also not surprise you enormously that I take a great delight in the vintage tractor show too, which is the biggest of its kind in Europe and brings hundreds of wonderful old machines – and old enthusiasts – together.

Rather more frustrating was my time on the managing board of the Newark Sports Association which was going to build a 12-acre sports hub with a running track, two football pitches, a cycle track, tennis courts and an administrative building. Unfortunately for us, the district council decided that the association which had been specifically created for the role didn't have the necessary expertise to complete the task and passed the development over to the YMCA.

They managed to construct a running track and two synthetic pitches (installed by my old company as it happens) but things were still looking a bit bleak. However, I am delighted to say it has now had a happy ending with the construction of a Community and Activity Village. The great news for Newark is that funding has come through and work started in 2021 on the main building which will be a really important amenity for all the people of the area. It's a lovely site and whether you're a dedicated athlete or a Sunday dog walker, there will be plenty of opportunities for everyone. Congratulations to everyone for their collective achievement.

As president of Newark and Nottinghamshire County Show (in my father's bowler hat) with my wife Vanessa and Professor Sir Michael Bond

Preparatory photo of me for a portrait by Nick McCann 2018

Having said that, I was able to lend a hand at one other local sports facility – the Newark Rugby Club. Now rugby was really Geoffrey's game, not mine, but they're a nice bunch of people and they came knocking one day to see if I would give them a few quid towards the new clubhouse. Now the way I see it, there is no harm in asking and, by and large, the British are pretty rubbish at asking for help – even when it comes to philanthropy. But when the rugby club came calling, I had to say well, you've got to come up with a shopping list and I can see if there is something that interests me.

So, they said they wanted to build a meeting room as part of the new clubhouse which they could let out on commercial terms to fund the activities of the club. Now, that is talking my language because it was a sensible business project with a definable budget and a recognisable outcome. In the end, that's what I went for and they very kindly put my name in gold letters on the door so that future generations can look at it, reflect and then pose the crucial question – who the bloody hell was he? On the really positive side though, it has proved really useful and has been hired out by the likes of Eon, the energy company.

Sorry if this sounds a 'look at me, aren't I generous' but it actually does fit my business philosophy that if you get a lot out of life, you absolutely have to put something back. Even though I have stated a couple of times that I never did this solely for the money, it is extremely rewarding to be able to help when it is necessary. That's why I decided to pay for the Lawrence bell which now rings in the beautiful All Saints church in the village of Hawton where I grew up and where my mother lived most of her life until she passed away in 2000.

You've probably never heard of All Saints Church but experts say it has some of the most magnificent medieval sculpture in Britain and it rivals some of the country's cathedrals for its elaborate style. Please pay it a visit and you won't be disappointed. While you're there, you might get lucky and hear the bells pealing and if your ears are attuned you will detect that along with the seven existing bells which date from the 16th century there is an eighth deeper sound to make a full octave – the Lawrence bell. The church has always been a treasure trove of memories dating from the time when my parents would attend Sunday services and my father would sing loudly and out of tune to every hymn and invariably say 'Amen' ahead of the rest of the congregation.

But it was largely in memory of my wonderful mother, that I decided to stump up for the big bell and it was great fun watching it being cast and then mounted in the spire. What's more, barring some cataclysmic geographical event, it will be still be ringing out its sombre note long after I am still around. It just tickles me that in centuries to come, my voice may have been silenced but the bell can speak for me.

No doubt I will get a chance to contribute to other worthwhile causes in the years to come but I really wanted to conclude with some general thoughts about how best to be effective as an entrepreneur and what, if anything, can be done to encourage and assist the would-be creators of the future. To be honest, I am deeply concerned for the young members of my family and youngsters in general, that paying for the COVID-19 crisis will be a loose noose around their necks for a long time to come. That's why it's more important than ever, to make sure that wealth creators are given the tools, trust and time to deliver their full potential.

Government certainly can't do it. A report from the highly respected international body the Organisation for Economic Cooperation and Development (OECD) concluded recently that while research and development spending by businesses drives growth, spending by government does not. The report said that trying to create innovation through a top-down approach simply doesn't work – and that absolutely resonates with all my half-century of experience in business. As the economist Milton Friedman put it: the business of business is business. Spot on.

To be honest, I don't think government does very much in any way to help budding entrepreneurs and in some ways that's a good thing. When I look at how much red tape and bureaucracy there is these days, I really don't think I would have been able to build the business I did. Don't get me wrong, I don't have a problem with health and safety issues, and I am proud to say that we never had a single serious injury at the plant even though recycling giant lorry tyres is an inherently dangerous business.

It's just that the safety official ends up having more power in the factory than the bloody managing director. If they want to, they can shut the whole plant down, no matter what the commercial pressures happen to be at that particular time. That just strikes me as putting the cart quite a few hundred meters ahead of the horse. Like I say, I was always acutely aware of the potential dangers but if I have a bunch of customers clamouring for raw materials, they have to be my first priority. If they weren't then there wouldn't be any factory for the safety gurus to shut down.

Perhaps the only other area where I think the government could create a more benign climate for the next generation of would-be entrepreneurs, is in the tax regime. In the past I have wagered everything – potentially even the roof over my head – to make sure the business had the finance it needed to invest and succeed. It always seemed to me that the tax system didn't reflect that risk element and it was only with the advent of COVID-19 that the government suddenly rushed out all kinds of support measures, interest free loans and furlough schemes which they would otherwise say were impossible.

Okay, I've had my little rant about how you could make this country even more encouraging for entrepreneurs, but I would also like to say that from a far more fundamental standpoint, this is and will remain a great country for doing business. The fact that for many years the UK was the biggest recipient of inward investment in Europe – I know France took the lead recently – is the best indicator of overseas faith in the country's economic future. And the reason I think that is the case, is that the British are basically an honest and straightforward bunch.

Again, don't get me wrong and think I am being rude about some of our European competitors, all I am saying is that when you are doing a deal in this country and your opposite number says we are good to go, then in my experience it will happen. You've got to get the lawyers in to do the small print and, as I've said, I would then go over the small print with a fine-tooth comb to make absolutely sure that the phrase 'liquidated damages' hadn't crept in. That was because even I couldn't control the weather so if the track installation was delayed, we didn't have to pay them damages. Eventually, they just stopped putting it in the contracts.

In general, I don't have a lot of time for politicians since I think their main interest in making a good steady living for themselves. That's not a party political or partisan view, I couldn't really give you tuppence for any of them. Though one notable exception is my friend and former cabinet minister John Selwyn Gummer – now Lord Deben. He has been incredibly helpful sorting out the rules governing the recycling industry and helped to persuade other European countries that recycled rubber was a product, and not waste, so it could be sold seamlessly throughout the European Union.

Now that's the kind of practical help which senior politicians can provide but which, in my experience, far too few do. What's more Lord Deben has remained extremely active on issues of climate change which is perfect for a former Secretary of State for the Environment. Personally, I'd rather poke my eyes out with sharp sticks than get involved with politics though I confess that I was once on the parish council of the village of Brant-Broughton – heady stuff, I hear you say.

Now the nice thing about writing your own book is that you are guaranteed the last word. Mine would be that fifty years ago, I would never have imagined that I would be where I am, half a century later. With a clear conscience, I can encourage any budding businesspeople that this is something that is fulfilling, demanding but hugely rewarding. I don't just mean having a couple of quid in the bank, I mean that you will meet some fascinating people, travel the world and build something you can legitimately be proud of.

One of the things I do is to go into Brackenhurst College at the University of Trent Nottingham. It's a huge countryside estate with a working farm, state-of-the-art teaching facilities, an equestrian centre and some of the best animal and land-based learning in the country. That's actually what they say about themselves, but I happen to agree. Nottingham Showground provides grants of £15,000 every year to students who show genuine enthusiasm and commitment and can explain what they will do with the grant if they get it.

There was one lad who came in for the interview, which decides whether or not they get the money, and he starts boasting about how his mother had brought him there in her BMW. Now do you think we gave him any money? Well, you're right there. But there was another chap who came in who was working as a bouncer in a nightclub to earn a living. However, he told us that all he had ever wanted to do was to breed pigs. He said he had rented a bit of land and that he found pigs utterly fascinating. He completely bowled me over with his commitment and you can bet he got a grant to help him pursue his dream. I really hope he is doing well.

You see I get a real kick out of persuading someone to follow their own dream – not something cooked up by their parents. Being part of the team allocating these grants forced me to think long and hard about who I am as a person. I know I'm known as a bit of an extrovert and I certainly don't mince my words, but I hope I have always blended that directness – some would call it bluntness – with a measure of humour and a lot of honesty. If something needs saying, then those who know me expect me to say it, even if there are consequences. That has stood me well in business and in life.

Maybe in some quarters that would be seen as rude or discourteous. Well I'm sorry, but I really don't think I am either of those, I am simply being honest. I always have been, and I know that I always will be. What you see is exactly what you get.

Postscript

Now it wouldn't be right if I didn't pass on my thanks to the person who has worked with me on this book and who, I am delighted to say, has become a good friend in the process.

Mark Webster is a journalist and broadcaster with many years of experience at the *Financial Times* and Independent Television News.

As ITN's business and economics editor, Moscow correspondent and Ireland bureau chief he's had a wide range of experience and has done a great job working with me.

Putting this volume together has not always been easy but we have had a lot of fun – and many laughs – throughout our time together.

We will now have to make up for the fact that we managed so few face-to-face conversations during the pandemic by socialising more in the years ahead.

Charles Lawrence